"Fo
The
dru
and
his kitchen stool in his home in Woody Creek, Michael Cleverly
and Bob Braudis have done a masterful job of presenting the
latter Hunter S. Thompson in *The Kitchen Readings*, a tale
of the smart, amusing, and passionate soul behind the Gonzo
mask. For anyone wanting to really understand the literary
impetus for such modern classics as *Fear and Loathing in Las
Vegas* and *The Curse of Lono*, this is a must read."

> —Loren Jenkins, Pulitzer Prize–winning journalist
> and senior foreign editor for National Public Radio

"*The Kitchen Readings* has many untold stories. . . . Another
important book for your library if you would like to learn
more about Hunter's life at Owl Farm from some of his closest
friends and neighbors. . . . I found it honest, refreshing, and
great fun."   —Deborah Fuller, longtime friend
> and personal assistant to the Good Doctor
> for twenty-three years

"I read the book on Halloween and it was frightening, as if I
had been visited by Hunter himself. Few people knew him as
well as Braudis and Cleverly, and they have preserved him in all
his treachery, foolishness, and wisdom. If Hunter were wearing
lipstick—their faces would be smeared with gratitude."

> —Bob Rafelson, award-winning writer-director
> of *Five Easy Pieces*

"There's Hunter Thompson the writer, Hunter Thompson the character, and Hunter Thompson the man. Most of us know the first two, but only a few can claim to have known the third. Here is a memoir of a deep four-decade friendship with one of America's national treasures. Braudis and Cleverly are the real deal, and they are natural storytellers. This book is hilarious, heartbreaking, and hard to put down."

—William McKeen, author of *Outlaw Journalist* and *Highway 61*

"Owl Farm really was the headquarters for the craziness and constant activity that was Hunter's life, and Cleverly and Braudis were flies on the wall for many of the most memorable high jinks. But more than that, they were also there when Hunter let down his guard. Hunter really was an inexplicable paradox—both self-consumed yet often extremely generous and sensitive—and Cleverly and Braudis captured that perfectly in their book. A triumphant tribute to a great friend."

—Tracy Keenan Wynn, Emmy Award–winning screenwriter

About the Authors

MICHAEL CLEVERLY is an Aspen-area artist who—though he tries to avoid confining definitions—prefers to think of himself as a pornographer. He has been writing a column for the *Aspen Times Weekly* since 2000. Cleverly has been married twice. He has two daughters, two ex-wives, a son-in-law, and a grandson named Oliver, and lives near a fortified compound in Woody Creek, Colorado.

SHERIFF BOB BRAUDIS has been the sheriff of Pitkin County, Colorado, since 1986. He spent eight years as an Aspen ski bum before economic reality hit and the custody of two preteen daughters forced him to seek steady employment as a deputy.

The Kitchen Readings

The Kitchen Readings

Untold Stories of Hunter S. Thompson

MICHAEL CLEVERLY and BOB BRAUDIS

HARPER PERENNIAL

NEW YORK ● LONDON ● TORONTO ● SYDNEY

THE KITCHEN READINGS. Copyright © 2008 by Michael Cleverly and Bob Braudis. All rights reserved. Printed in the United States of America. No part of this book may be used or reproduced in any manner whatsoever without written permission except in the case of brief quotations embodied in critical articles and reviews. For information address HarperCollins Publishers, 10 East 53rd Street, New York, NY 10022.

HarperCollins books may be purchased for educational, business, or sales promotional use. For information please write: Special Markets Department, Harper-Collins Publishers, 10 East 53rd Street, New York, NY 10022.

FIRST EDITION

Designed by Justin Dodd

Library of Congress Cataloging-in-Publication Data

Cleverly, Michael.
    The kitchen readings : untold stories of Hunter S. Thompson / Michael Cleverly and Bob Braudis.—1st Harper Perennial ed.
        p. cm.
    ISBN: 978-0-06-115928-2
    1. Thompson, Hunter S. 2. Thompson, Hunter S.—Friends and associates. 3. Authors, American—Twentieth century—Biography.
I. Braudis, Bob. II. Title.
PS3570.H62Z65 2008
813'.54—dc22
    [B]   2007040133

08 09 10 11 12   ID/RRD   10 9 8 7 6 5 4 3 2 1

This book is dedicated to the memory
of our dear friend
Tom Benton

Introduction

The title *The Kitchen Readings* refers to Hunter's writing process. He loved to hear his own words read aloud. He would write; his friends would read. This is how he edited, how his work evolved . . . on into the night. That process took place in the kitchen at Owl Farm, Hunter's home in Woody Creek, Colorado. The kitchen was the center of life at Owl Farm and it was the engine room for Hunter's literary juggernaut. The kitchen may indeed be the hub of many American homes—and though life at Owl Farm was Hunter S. Thompson's life, it certainly was not traditional American fare, nor was it quite the life that might be imagined by the many thousands of Hunter's fans. Hunter made himself the hero of his books. He also manipulated the tools of the information age to create a mystique that stood apart from his writing. Hunter has a huge base of people who love his writing and a second, perhaps even larger, fan base of people who are drawn to his mystique. Hunter's admirers base their knowledge of him on three sources: his writings, the image he crafted in his writing and projected in his life, and the almost endless stream of superficial profiles created by journalists who would briefly visit Owl Farm and rush home to crank out their "Hunter Thompson in Woody Creek" story.

Doc, Cleverly, and artists Mary Conover and Earl Biss enjoy a quiet evening in the kitchen.

Over the years, we have watched Owl Farm visitors come and go, the famous and the forever unknown, celebrities and artists, intellectuals and fools. Many of them took a turn reading in the kitchen, and we were there. We were part of Hunter's life on a daily basis.

Pitkin County sheriff Bob Braudis, one of your narrators, was Hunter's closest confidant for many years. He was told that he had earned the right to "show up anytime" without invitation or notice, a reward for loyalty, professional problem solving, and tolerance. Hunter intimidated most people, but not the sheriff. Hunter and Bob came to each other as equals, and this created a healthy atmosphere that they both relished.

Hunter would use Bob to ease the tension during difficult business negotiations, or anytime, in fact, that it was to Hunter's advantage for a guest in the kitchen to remain calm and unterrified. How bad could things get with the sheriff there? Bob would also act as interpreter. It took years for Hunter's friends to get used to his mumble. Learning his language would occur through some sort of weird osmosis over a long period of time. At some point it would simply dawn on you that you could understand every word that Hunter was saying, while those around you were just staring at him and nodding or scratching their heads. First you'd ponder just how the hell this had happened, and then you'd begin to worry about what exactly it meant. Both Bill Murray and Johnny Depp managed to find a way to mimic Hunter's speech while keeping it intelligible, an astounding feat, but not one Hunter was interested in duplicating. Bob Braudis was fluent in Hunter's mumblese and would fill the interpreter role with diplomacy and charm. He could be counted on to keep to himself what transpired, and to offer an intelligent, objective perspective when needed.

In the 1970s, Hunter was in and out of the Roaring Fork Valley looking for stories, and he actually wrote some of them. Bob would always be there when Hunter returned, to give him the inside scoop on whatever had happened at home during his absence and to provide an honest sounding board for Hunter's tales of his own adventures. The two men who rarely needed backup from anyone could lean on each other. Bob says that if you held his feet to the fire he'd have to say that Hunter gave him more than he gave Hunter, but neither of them kept a ledger.

Bob Braudis has been Pitkin County sheriff for the last twenty years and was recently elected to another term. Before that, he spent nearly a decade as a sheriff's deputy and two years as a county commissioner. Bob came to Aspen seeking the life of a ski bum, but the ski bum life is that of a single man, and Bob had a family. After eight years he finally surrendered and found a "straight" job. That job was in law enforcement, and the rest is history.

Courtesy of Deborah Fuller

Cleverly enjoying a beverage
with Doc on the deck, perhaps
straining to understand the words
coming out of Hunter's mouth.

Karl Wolfgang

Sheriff Braudis, not showing the
strain of his friendships with
Cleverly and Thompson.

Your other narrator, artist Michael Cleverly, migrated to Aspen in the early seventies. Back then, Aspen was a classic ski town and still retained some of the charming qualities of small-town America. Aspen's artists and writers were an intimate community, and it would have been impossible for Cleverly and Hunter not to meet. In fact, Cleverly's studio was in the *Aspen Times* building, right next to the Hotel Jerome and its famous "J-Bar." A hardworking painter needs a break sometimes, and quite often Hunter would be at the far end of the bar having "office hours." Cleverly and Hunter shared many interests, and the two became close. Later Cleverly would move to a cabin in Woody Creek, just up the road from Owl Farm. Already friends, when they became neighbors Cleverly and Thompson found their contact evolving into an almost daily (or nightly) event. Hunter had someone he could trust just minutes away, and that meant a lot to him. Cleverly spent more waking hours in Hunter's kitchen than in his own living room.

The stage for the earliest stories in this book is Aspen, Colorado. In the 1970s the J-Bar was the hip gathering place in Aspen. Movie stars mingled with construction workers, wealthy trust-funders with ski bums. There was a wonderful democracy about the town in general, and the J-Bar in particular. It was a comfortable atmosphere for artists and writers, and it was where we spent our "off" hours. It became the clubhouse. "The J-Bar" was our name for what was officially "The Bar at the Hotel Jerome." Happy hour was "roll call," and attendance was required. If you didn't show up, people worried and got on the phone. The bar was the scene of many legendary events, and of some stories that can't be told even decades later. Our friend Michael Solheim ran the place, the waitresses were all young and beautiful, and the bartenders were our buddies. It was a happy family of people whose only common denominator might have been their madness. Our gatherings there went on for years, maybe a little longer than they should have. We began to lose friends to rehab and jail. Eventually the hotel renamed it "The J-Bar" and lettered that on the windows. By then we had pretty much stopped going there. We gave it up to the next generation and the principal action moved down valley, to the Woody Creek Tavern.

The Tavern was located just over a mile from Owl Farm, so getting home from there was a lot safer than driving all the way

back from Aspen after a hard night. The only word in the English language that begins to describe the décor of the Tavern is *eclectic*, but that doesn't really do it. The slightly decaying Victorian opulence of the J-Bar was easy to envision; the Tavern was the polar opposite. The walls were covered with photographs, and news-

Courtesy of Cheryl Frymire

Legendary Tavern bartender Steve Bennet and waitress Cheryl Frymire with young Bob and Doc; Cleverly with friend and neighbor Sue Carrolan. Sue was at Owl Farm with Cleverly the Friday night before Hunter died.

Waitress Cheryl with Doc and Johnny Depp. The Tavern staff got a little mileage out of the celebrities who visited.

paper and magazine clippings that went several layers deep. The visual chaos made it impossible for the eye to rest on the few pieces of framed art that shared the wall space. The place was basically an insult to Aspen snootiness; it looked as if the interior decorating decisions had been made with an eye toward withstanding a chair-swinging barroom brawl rather than to make the customers feel special. The fact that it was located in the middle of a trailer park was perfectly consistent with its overall "no-frills" working-class ambience. Of course, by the time Hunter died, Woody Creek had seen its fair share of celebrities move in, along with the building of monster homes by the superrich. But in the beginning the Tavern was a place for regular folks, where Aspen types came on safari, and Hunter was king.

The Kitchen Readings are tales of events that took place in the Jerome, the Tavern, and, of course, the Owl Farm kitchen. There are also stories that take us to exotic locales, such as Vietnam during the fall of Saigon, Grenada as the U.S. invades, and New Orleans with its pub crawls and transsexuals. The stories are compiled from our own recollections and those of Hunter's other close friends and neighbors, people who tend to keep their memories private, but who disinterred them for us. The stories span a period from 1968, when Hunter first arrived in Woody Creek, delivering a load of furniture for art dealer Patricia Moore, to the day of his death. They deal with his 3:00 A.M. phone calls to discuss vital, urgent, matters such as . . . firewood—and the 5:00 A.M. drive-bys, with Hunter leaning on the horn in the predawn darkness and pitching explosives out the window of his car. His idiosyncrasies and bizarre habits are explored at length and in depth. We'll both be writing first-person accounts of our adventures with Hunter, so we'll identify who's speaking (Braudis or Cleverly) at the beginning of the chapters. The stories that are a result of our interviews with others close to Hunter are written in the third person.

The kitchen in Hunter's cabin at Owl Farm was a simple knotty-pine affair, both the walls and the cabinets. A few years ago the pine cabinets were replaced with cherry, but the walls remained knotty pine, with vintage orange shellac. Hunter's famous counter stretched across two thirds of the kitchen. Behind the counter sat Hunter, and behind Hunter were the range, the sink, countertop, and assorted cutting boards. Cooking on the range essentially put you back to back with Hunter, a dubious honor or a dangerous position, depending on his mood. The couch was backed up against the front of the counter so everyone was facing the same direction: the TV. The only other stool at the counter, besides Hunter's, was just to Hunter's left. That stool was always occupied by the person highest in Hunter's pecking order, the sheriff, if he was in attendance. The regulars knew to vacate it when a higher-ranking crony entered the kitchen; newcomers had to be told. Next to that stool was an exercise bicycle. Ostensibly it was there so Hunter could just hop on and get a bunch of exercise, Hunter not being one to go charging off to the gym. It must be reported that Hunter had been seen on the thing, but exercise isn't the word to describe what he was doing. We old-timers weren't too fond of it, but younger guests thought it was pretty cool and would cheerfully jump on and pedal away. There was one easy chair that also faced the TV. Next to the television was the upright piano; in all those years, no one seems to remember ever having heard one note out of it. When Hunter was working on a major project he'd have a large corkboard hung in front of the piano, which would fill up with notes for the book, as well as random aphorisms and bits of pornography. The kitchen would morph to meet the requirements of the event at hand, with more furniture being hauled in so the maximum number of people could be jammed in to watch the Kentucky Derby, Super Bowl, or perhaps presidential debates.

The living room was through the door next to the piano. It was a nice large room, especially considering Hunter's cabin wasn't particularly huge. A big fieldstone fireplace dominated one end. The wall to the right, as you entered from the kitchen, had the front door and picture windows looking out on the deck and the peacock cage. The room was full of books, plus stuffed animals, skulls, and the sort of exotic memorabilia that people associate with Hunter S. Thompson.

An old friend, who goes way back with Hunter, explained why that big comfortable room wasn't the center of activity at Owl Farm. It started years ago, when Hunter was between girl-friends and couldn't afford someone to keep house for him. Everyone used to hang out in the living room, but it got to a point where no one had cleaned it up for weeks, maybe months, and it had devolved into an utterly squalid, fetid, pigsty. There were decaying turkey carcasses, which were convenient to snack on for the first few days but started to smell like corpses after a while. Half-eaten ham sandwiches lying around that you'd remember as having been in the same place on

Courtesy of Paul Chelsey

Election Night was always huge at Owl Farm. Some ended well. Some not so well. I think Hunter just kept the pool money from the 2000 election that took so long to resolve.

your last visit, and all the other general trash and debris of daily living. Hunter didn't have a very good sense of smell; maybe he was just oblivious to all of it. Ultimately it was easier to just move to the kitchen than it would have been to tackle that god-awful mess. Once the scene moved into the kitchen, it never moved back.

For the big Kentucky Derby and Super Bowl parties, the TV from Hunter's bedroom would be hauled into the living room. The buffet would be set up in there, and that's where the overflow would watch the game. Those of us who spent as much time in Doc's kitchen as we did our own homes would often opt for the living room, as the kitchen would fill up with acolytes and first-timers desperate to be close to him.

Usually the people assembled at Owl Farm fit quite comfortably into the kitchen. When things became uncomfortable there, it wasn't due to overcrowding; that would have been too simple. It was because *someone* was making things uncomfortable. It was something Hunter was very good at.

The good folk of Woody Creek were proud of the fact that Hunter Thompson called their little village home. Woody Creekers are famous for having a set of values different than those of the people up the road in Aspen, and they go out of their way to demonstrate it every chance they get. They embraced Hunter, and he was a good neighbor. He didn't care if you were of the same political stripe as he was, or if you shared his hobbies or leisure-time activities; being a neighbor was different from being a crony; a neighbor was a neighbor no matter what. That feeling was reciprocated. People who were political opposites of Hunter, who would never have joined us in the kitchen for a game or other dubious behavior, felt very warm toward him because they knew he truly was a good neighbor who was cordial and courteous and could be counted on if he were needed.

Hunter felt safe in Woody Creek. Those around him always respected his privacy and would insulate him from outsiders who might try to intrude. You could never get directions to Owl Farm from a Tavern bartender. If a pilgrim set on meeting Hunter seemed overly persistent, a call would be made and someone, such as Cleverly, would appear to do the screening. It would be explained to the individual that he hadn't been asked to come to Woody Creek, and that the thousands of miles that he might have traveled to worship at the altar of "gonzo" were irrelevant. Doc wasn't interested. If a reasonable chat didn't work, there was always the Sheriff.

No matter how exotic or glamorous Hunter's journeys, he always looked forward to his return to Owl Farm, Woody Creek, and the company of his small circle of trusted friends. These are their stories. These tales aren't necessarily the outrageous "gonzo" stuff that people tend to write, and that fans expect to read, about Hunter. Often funny, sometimes poignant, these stories are the real Hunter, the private Hunter. Hunter was a gentleman; he would always rise when a woman entered the room and would always greet someone new with courtesy and decorum. Hunter was a well-bred Southerner with good manners, and that was important to him. When, upon occasion, those manners weren't apparent, it wasn't because he'd forgotten them. He could also be the madman his fans envisioned, the one portrayed in film and in Ralph Steadman's brilliant illustrations. He was also a friend, a husband, and a father.

We're writing this book to show the many sides of Hunter— the Hunter Thompson who was unavailable to anyone but those closest to him. Even if other writers thought that these were qualities of Doc's they wanted to explore, they couldn't have; they wouldn't have had the access, and now never will.

The Kitchen Readings

Two Beginnings

CLEVERLY DISCUSSES COCAINE AND TITS AS BIG AS TEXAS

It's funny that I don't remember the first time I met Hunter. I had read *Hell's Angels* and *Fear and Loathing in Las Vegas* before moving to Aspen, so I was well aware of who Hunter Thompson was. I remember seeing him on his stool at the end of the Jerome Bar. But for all that, I can't remember our first real encounter. Maybe I can blame this memory lapse on the seventies; maybe someone was on something. It's likely we were introduced by our mutual friend Tom Benton. Tom is the artist who designed Hunter's GONZO fist logo and also the original cover for *Fear and Loathing on the Campaign Trail,* the one with the stars-and-stripes skull. Tom worked on Hunter's sheriff's campaign and created the "Aspen Wall Posters," which were a large part of the PR blitz for that campaign. Tom and Hunter were very good friends and had a mutual respect. As it turned out, Tom and I spent a lot of the seventies and eighties driving the same galleries out of business. It was hard work; we became close. It's likely that at some point he was the one who first put Hunter and me together.

My first real recollection, my first Hunter story, was an encounter that took place at the far end of the Jerome Bar in the mid-1970s. Hunter was perched on his stool; I was on the stool next to him. By now we had become friendly. Friendly enough to share drinks, conversation, whatever else. We were doing just that when a young couple approached with caution. Hippies. I thought I'd left you guys back in Vermont.

It was mid-afternoon on a beautiful sunny day. It was far too nice out for good people to be in a saloon. So it was just Hunter, me, the bartender, a couple of real estate agents scheming in a distant corner, and the hippies. The guy was a furry little fellow, standard hippie-issue fare. The girl was hot. She had great Texas-size breasts swelling out against her hippie top, which did a terrible job of covering them, cleavage to the wind. Hunter chose not to ignore them, the hippies, for two obvious reasons.

"Hi," the hippies said. It turned out that they were on a pilgrimage, and Hunter was it. They had traveled some distance to meet the great man, and now they were here. And here he was.

"Hi," Hunter responded. "No, no, not disturbing us at all, just having a little lunch," he said, eyes glued on Texas.

Hippie ears were cocked, trying to figure what the hell Hunter was saying. This was a classic response for those chatting with Doc for the first time. Or the thousandth. There was plenty of adoration to go around, and Hunter graciously accepted every ounce of it. He even went so far as to show some interest in them, while mentally willing those young breasts closer and closer to him. He had somehow maneuvered the hippie girl between us and now had his arm around her. I was enjoying her smell. The target area was pointed directly at Doc.

Suddenly the guy edged very close. "Hey," he whispered, "you guys want a bump?"

Only one answer to that question.

"Where do we go?" the hippie asked.

"Right here's fine," Hunter said.

It was the seventies in Aspen. We thought the stuff was legal; we thought it was good for you. None of our friends had been hauled off to rehab yet. Hippie boy produced a vial, chock full. Yum, yum. Hunter reached out and snatched it from his hand like a striking cobra. Lightning fast.

He unscrewed the top and held it up to the light, then proceeded to dump out a large pile of cocaine onto the top of each of the young lady's breasts. Both hippies were frozen, mouths agape. I watched, waiting for Hunter to produce a bill to roll up, or some other cocaine-snorting device. None was forthcoming. Hunter proceeded to place a finger over one nostril and bury his face into one of the breasts, making loud snarfling sounds with liberal flashes of tongue. The pile of cocaine disappeared. He repeated the process, covering the other nostril and snarfling the other breast. When he pulled his face away from the girl's bosom, his nose and upper lip were smeared with the white powder. Saliva glistened around his mouth.

He held the vial up to the light again: about a quarter full. He handed it to me. I dumped the remainder of the substance onto the back of my hand and snorted it the same way Hunter had, but unfortunately sans breast. My pulse quickened and there was a pleasant sensation, though I still was pretty sure that Hunter had had the most fun.

I handed the vial back to Hunter. He held it up again, empty. He screwed the top back on and tossed it to the hippie boy. The hippies stared, mouths hanging open, the girl's cleavage soaked with Hunter's spit. What had just happened?

Hunter turned to me, his back to the hippies, and resumed our conversation at exactly the point where the young couple had interrupted it. They lingered; they had only Hunters back. Then the boy took the girl's arm, and they slowly retreated. Backing up, then turning to the door. They had met Hunter S. Thompson. Did we get their names? Did they get mine? Did we know where they were going, where they came from? They were gone, perhaps off on their next quest.

BRAUDIS REMEMBERS ROUGH AND TUMBLE: PAVEMENT AND POLITICS

My earliest memories are of pavement. South Boston, 1948. Concrete sidewalks and tar streets. Blacktop playgrounds. In the winter people scattered ashes from their coal furnaces on the ice so they wouldn't slip. I remember one cold day being pulled on a sled by my mother. I remember the metal runners screeching over the ash and clinkers. I was bundled in a hooded snowsuit with one ear sticking out. My mother took a shortcut across a vacant lot and a twig got stuck in my eye. As I cried I saw my mother's guilt.

Today, as I gaze out the window at the Elk Mountain range, there is no tar in sight. I came here to ski. Back in Boston, we played hockey on a frozen pond at Farragut Park. Shin guards were copies of the *Boston Globe* friction-taped to my legs. I was a good skater and a good fighter. When I first tried skiing in Vermont I was a natural.

I outgrew the gangs and the juvenile crime. I briefly believed in our government. I married and sired two daughters. I copped a corporate job and thought I was happy. We owned a Ford Country Squire station wagon and a VW bug.

Wasn't this the life everyone wanted? Maybe, but I had this coppery taste in my mouth because of the war in Vietnam.

Instead of baiting cops for sport in Southie, I was shedding the three-piece pinstripes on weekends and getting tear-gassed in antiwar demonstrations. The seeds of rebellion from Boston bloomed in New York. Dope replaced Beefeater, Levi Strauss supplanted Brooks Brothers, and my rail out of the East was greased. I arrived in Colorado to ski. No purpose was the new purpose. Tell me not to do it and I'll do it. Good Jesuit gone awry.

The Teutonic establishment in Aspen was postwar Swiss and Austrian. Never German by admission. We were the new-comers, the outsiders, postgrad hippies and a threat to the status quo and the bottom line. Our growing ranks might hurt real estate values. We thought we could save the Rocky Mountains from those who saw only the bottom line.

I had seen Hunter at the bar in the Hotel Jerome. I had read about his battles against the city council and the municipal court. His group was a loose alliance

Courtesy of Aspen Productions

Young Braudis, as a rookie, taking advantage of Aspen's social scene.

of artists, lawyers, writers, and shady imports with no visible means of support. They had their end of the long bar.

My bunch skied every day and self-medicated with whatever was handy. We all converged at the Jerome. Without any clear introduction, Hunter and I started calling each other by name. Osmosis by whiskey. Eight nights a week.

Jesus! It seems as though everyone who knew Hunter met him at the Jerome. Its high ceiling, tile floor, and grand Victorian back bar made it a great place to drink. As the sides were forming in the Battle of Aspen, the office of sheriff was Hunter's choice for his first beachhead. In the United States of America the office of sheriff is the only chief law enforcement position controlled by the voters.

That spring the snow was melting, the lifts were closed, jobs had ended, and relationships were difficult. As frozen horse shit thawed, not a tourist was to be found. The climate for conversation was good, and I found my stool was getting closer to Hunter's. I listened to Doc and his brain trust formulate a plan. Hunter saw the opportunity. Power resided with the people. Freaks were people, and more of us arrived every day. If we registered and if we voted, we just might outnumber the complacent conservatives in November. "Freak power" was the surge, and HST had the courage to ride that wave.

Hunter had crafted a platform that might have seemed an odd match for the office he was seeking. He spoke to land use, zoning, and greed control. The sheriff in Hunter's model would become an ombudsman. He declared that as sheriff of Pitkin County, he would change the name of the city of Aspen to "Fat City." Everything he said that summer appealed to me. I enlisted as a foot soldier in my first real crusade. I understood guns and badges, but what the hell did growth control have to do with a sheriff? Hunter knew the answer to that question. He was a highly evolved student of essential political matters. In 1958, in *The Rum Diary,* he described the threat posed by greedy land developers by stating that, unchecked, they "spread like piss puddles in a parking lot." At age twenty-one, he grasped the reality

Richard Shenk Photo

Courtesy of Marci Benton

Bob's campaigns have been consistently more successful than Hunter's.

that it was always greed versus the environment.

What might have appeared to an outsider in 1970 as Thompson's brainless rant against the machine was actually his refined statement about the art of controlling one's environment. That year Hunter already had the powerful magnetism that lasted

The brilliant artist Tom Benton designed posters for both Hunter and Braudis. Both are much-sought-after collectibles.

until his death. As the nucleus for an embryonic political force that shook Aspen's establishment, Hunter infected a small group of future candidates with a fever that eventually led to victories that we shared with him.

For most of us, that campaign, filled with passion and some tears, was the political apogee. But the friendships and loyalties that Hunter cemented gave some traction—not unlike those ashes on the ice in my old 'hood—to subsequent campaigns that gave life to the original agenda that the Doc connected to the concept called quality of life.

Following his loss in November, I remember Hunter asking me about the informal power-up model of gang structure. It was as if he were taking mental notes. I had gone from dean's list to dropout; but now Hunter told me that his foray into politics had exposed weaknesses in the comfortable oligarchy of Aspen. I was starting to feel my part in what Hunter foresaw. Despite the "Carpe Noctum" existentialism and the denial of death and tomorrow, Hunter persuaded me and other supporters to view his loss on Election Day as the beginning, not the end, of "Freak Power."

The curtain was rising on the Gonzo Years, the hyperbole and craziness, but the pendulum was creeping toward its position of natural repose, with the Doc's hand in touch. He was to become, for me, a polestar and a conscience. Thirty-five years later he was a sharp twig in my eye.

Cleverly Chats with the Doctor

There's really no other way to put it. Facts are facts. Hunter mumbled. In short staccato bursts. The way they teach you to use a fully automatic weapon. A quick spray, then another, then another. Covering the field. His mind was so quick that he had his words processed and considered before he could get them out. When the rest of us speak before we think, it gets us in trouble. For Hunter it was just the opposite. He couldn't get the words out fast enough, and his pauses were semicolons, not commas. Besides, he didn't give a hoot and a holler what anyone thought anyway.

Our ability to comprehend Hunter—or not—was our problem, not Hunter's. I don't think that I ever witnessed him make an effort to clarify himself. For some reason, none of this deterred TV hosts from courting him for their talk shows, or colleges from begging him to come lecture. Though these weren't Hunter's favorite activities, it wasn't because he was worried about people not understanding him—like I said, he really couldn't care less. What he didn't like was the structure of the things. In agreeing to them, he actually had to be somewhere at a certain time. You might say that tardiness was a shortcoming of Hunter's. People constantly forgave him this small flaw, I think, because it was so remarkable that he showed up at all. I suspect that the reason that he showed up was because he had some sort of agreement with his publisher—you know, the kind of agreement that's in writing, attended by lawyers, and signed with blood. That, plus I think the dough was pretty good on the lecture circuit. Money is always a wonderful motivator. Hunter tried to keep his lectures down to questions and answers; the way most people end their talks was how Hunter began his. He usually ended them by felonious assault with a handy fire extinguisher.

A few years ago I was sitting in a state of non-Zen nothingness and it occurred to me that at some unknown point I had become able to understand every word that Hunter said. How long had it been since I leaned closer in an effort to turn the sounds into words? I couldn't say. This epiphany kind of unnerved me. What did it mean? Was I spending too much time at Owl Farm? Was my ear–brain continuum evolving in some strange way? Was it the drugs? Nah. Couldn't be the drugs. I concluded that it didn't mean anything. I come to that conclusion a lot. It's safe.

Still, it did get me thinking, and took me back to the Jerome Bar years before, to what might have been my first one-on-one conversation with Doc, when we were just getting to know each other.

I walked into the place in mid-afternoon. Hunter was sitting at the bar having lunch. As usual he had ordered half the menu and was picking at the food. He had all the beverage bases covered as well: a Bloody Mary, a beer, a glass of water, and a tumbler of Chivas. Apparently some doofus had spotted Hunter just before I arrived. The doofus was dancing around the room, table to table, pointing out, "That's Hunter Thompson over there." Everyone loves that stuff. Figuring me as his only potential ally, Hunter asked me to join him. I sat down, and he said to help myself to some lunch. He had enough in front of him to feed two or three. He ordered me a beer, and I started picking around the different plates the same way he was. The doofus began to hover closer and closer and finally sat down next to us. Doc explained how he and I were in the middle of an important meeting and could really use some privacy. The guy actually took the hint and drifted off.

Doc and I started chatting, both of us relieved that we didn't have to deal with the fool. We talked and drank and grazed over the food, with me occasionally leaning close to make sure that I wasn't missing any Hunter Thompson wisdom. I thought it was going all right; sure, I'd miss some stuff here and there, but I believed I was keeping up. That is, I thought that I was keeping up until Hunter really took the ball and started to run with it. Now he was doing all the talking; I was merely audience. I listened carefully to every word, straining to understand, with only intermittent success. Nodding and smiling when I hoped it was appropriate, half comprehending, half bluffing. It seemed to be working. Hunter went on and on. One of us was having a great conversation. I started to get nervous about what would happen if, all of a sudden, Hunter required a reply from me. No need to fret; Doc was happy. He continued.

Finally he stopped dead. He fixed me with a hard, searching look. "Michael," he said, "you're the most unflappable person I've ever talked to." I am? My God, I thought, what the hell have we been talking about? The possibilities raced through my brain. Everything from sedition to loaning him my wife. "Hunter," I confessed, "I'm sorry. I haven't understood a word you've said for the last five minutes." Hunter gave me a kindly smile. I knew it was all right because it wasn't about me.

The doofus was gone, and we had finished our drinks and Hunter's lunch. We bade each other a good afternoon and promised to do this again soon.

Bob Tells Us About Maria and Lost Love

Hunter and Maria lived together for several years; but by 1987 Maria Khan had left the farm. A beautiful girl of Pakistani descent from a prominent Phoenix family, Maria finally decided that she had completed her enlistment as Hunter's live-in, sleep-in administrative assistant. Her black hair and gray/blue eyes probably accounted for part of Hunter's attraction to her, but she was also very smart. Smart enough to know it was time to return to Phoenix to continue her education.

Her parents despised Hunter, and although he knew it, he had difficulty accepting it. He retaliated by writing a gonzo exposé of the Khan clan in the Sunday supplement of a prominent Phoenix newspaper. This resulted in a serious widening of the Thomp-

Courtesy of Darryl Weaver

Maria and Hunter in happier times, joined on the links by David McCumber, Tex, Deb Fuller, and a pro.

son/Khan chasm. His charges against the Khans were borderline libel, but in some sense funny—particularly if you knew that part of Hunter's motivation was revenge for the family's supporting Maria's escape from Woody Creek. She had moved out unexpectedly, and Hunter was having trouble locating the particular straw that broke the back of the relationship. Certainly there had been some behavior issues, but nothing that dovetailed with the time immediately preceding her departure. Perhaps he deserved it, but in a just and fair universe there'd be an explanation, a measure of understanding. There'd be a straw.

After Maria left him, Hunter had been sent to Phoenix on assignment with the *San Francisco Examiner* to cover the Evan Mecham impeachment hearings.

Evan Mecham had run for governor of Arizona three times before finally being elected in 1986. After one short year in office, a recall effort was under way. An archconservative with megalo-maniacal tendencies, he had canceled Martin Luther King Day, defended the use of the word *pickaninny,* along with other racist slurs, and had declared the editor of the *Phoenix Gazette,* John Kolbe, a nonperson.

Mecham's whacko, loose-cannon style had cost the state of Arizona plenty of money, which was a matter that even those who could have forgiven those other little missteps couldn't ignore. Some estimates claim that his behavior cost the state as much as five hundred million dollars, including two hundred million in revenues when the NFL decided to pull the Super Bowl out of Phoenix. A recall petition was circulated garnering twice the necessary number of signatures. An election was scheduled, but before it could be held, impeachment proceedings were begun. Mecham was accused of concealing $350,000 in campaign con-tributions, and misusing state funds with an $80,000 state loan to Mecham Pontiac, a dealership owned by you know who. It was a made-for–Hunter Thompson kind of story.

When Hunter arrived in Phoenix he immediately called Maria, and she refused to see him. There was nothing left for him to do but invite me and a couple of other Aspen guys to join him for a few rounds of golf. When I got to his room at a Scotts-dale resort, he had rearranged it, tearing off some wainscoting in an effort to find a receptacle that would accept the plug of his IBM Selectric typewriter. He had just ordered $160 worth of shrimp cocktails and two bottles of champagne, two bottles of Chivas, and two cases of beer. The place looked like a landfill. In one corner of the mess was his golf bag. He didn't have a travel-ing case for the bag, so he'd wrapped the top with two blankets and used about a roll of duct tape to keep the clubs in the bag. His rental car—a convertible, of course—had been delivered but not released to him because his driver's license had expired.

While Maria boycotted his visit to Arizona, her brother, Bobby, who didn't share the Khan loathing for Hunter, responded to an invitation. When he came into the hotel room, Bobby said hello as Hunter was untaping his golf bag. Hunter opened a zippered pouch, pulled out a nine-millimeter semiautomatic pistol, and flipped it across the room to Bobby. Bobby fielded it, and Hunter said, "Nice catch," adding, "That's the best way to get a gun on an airplane."

When the phone rang, Hunter asked me to answer. It was Willie Hearst, Hunter's editor at the *Examiner*. I had often run interference for Hunter with Hearst, especially in reference to deadlines. This time he was questioning the room service charges, the still-parked rental car, and the lack of reports on the impeachment. I told Hearst that Hunter had taken a cab to the hearings venue and that I would tell him to call the *Examiner* on his return. I lied.

Hunter eventually submitted his coverage of one of the juiciest political scandals in recent memory without ever leaving the hotel. Another in a long list of hotel rooms was utterly destroyed. Maria didn't visit, and we never got Hunter to the golf course.

A few months later, Hunter used his wiles to convince Maria to come back to Colorado for a long weekend to attend his son Juan's graduation, summa cum laude, Phi Beta Kappa, from the University of Colorado. This was the only sort of bait that could work on Maria. Juan was a huge source of pride for Hunter, his ex-wife Sandy, Juan's mother, and everyone in their orbit. People were willing to accept the smallest scrap of credit for how well he had turned out, and did their best to conceal their amazement at his achievements. Juan hadn't grown up in a normal household.

Despite the unimaginable strangeness of being a child at Owl Farm, Juan was an excellent student from the get-go. He attended The Aspen Community School during his primary years. The Community School was an extremely liberal, progressive private institution located just up the hill from the farmhouse. Some might have called it a hippie school. The school gave over an inordinate portion of its academic year to the school play, and had spawned successful actors such as Oliver Platt and Felicity Huffman. Juan, too, was an emerging talent. At that time, a friend of Hunter's named Paul Rubin was directing most of the plays.

Paul Rubin's taste in theater was adult and sophisticated. He never let the fact that his cast and crew were schoolchildren affect his choices. He never pandered to the kids. Paul directed them in Eugene O'Neil's *Desire Under the Elms,* in *One Flew Over the Cuckoo's Nest,* and in James Baldwin's *Blues for Mr. Charlie.* Juan Thompson always had good roles. In *Blues,* he had the male lead, Preacher; the female lead, Juanita, was played by Thea Bent, the cute blond daughter of a well-loved Aspen physician. *Blues for Mr. Charlie* was performed by the cast of whiter-than-white Aspen kids in blackface. Thea wore a huge black frizzy wig. I'm not sure if even Woody Creek was ready for Paul Rubin, but you can see why he and Hunter got along.

Acting and academics were Juan's strengths; sports, not so much, so he was just about the perfect Community School student, as academics and the arts were what the parents were interested in. They didn't give a hoot about jock stuff, except maybe skiing.

The last two weeks of rehearsal before opening night, the kids' asses belonged to Rubin. They'd rehearse all day in groups and individually. When the kids weren't rehearsing, they'd get a pickup co-ed softball game together. Paul noticed that Juan didn't own a glove; he always had to borrow one. One weekend, Hunter and Paul were having lunch at the Jerome Bar. Hunter stopped in mid-conversation and looked up. "Tomorrow's Juan's birthday"—seemingly something just remembered. "What am I going to get him?" Doc had instantly made this Paul's project. Sensible, since Paul was spending more time with the kids than their parents were at that point. Paul thought. "A baseball glove. Juan doesn't have one; he always has to borrow one." Doc was ecstatic. Sports had always been so much a part of Hunter's life, and Juan had always leaned toward the academic. Hunter bolted from the J-Bar and down the block to Carl's Pharmacy, not just close but maybe the only place to purchase a ball glove in Aspen in those days.

On Monday it was back to school and rehearsals. Paul kept his eye out for the first sign of a softball game. When he saw bats and balls being rounded up, he told the kids he was working with to take five and he sought out Juan. Paul caught up with him on the side of the field. "How'd you like your birthday present?" he asked with pride, knowing he was the author of the idea. Juan looked down at the palms of his gloveless hands, then looked up into Paul's eyes and, with a sardonic smile, said, "I'm left-handed."

And yet, somehow, the combination of the Community School and Owl Farm had bred a young man who was graduating from CU with highest honors.

Hunter sent Maria a round-trip ticket to Aspen, and they drove to Boulder for Juan's commencement.

When Hunter and Maria returned to Woody Creek, he hid her purse and return ticket. He was de facto holding her hostage. Just after lunch one day, Maria called my office at the county courthouse and asked me to help her escape. She had a plane to catch in two hours.

She told me she was sitting on the bus stop bench outside the Woody Creek Tavern. Hunter was inside, at the bar. She said his house was locked tight, doors and windows, and she needed help. She emphasized that only I could possibly help. She didn't want any "official" intervention. With chivalry in my heart and no fear of Hunter, I drove down to the Tavern and talked to Maria. Then I went inside and saw Hunter at the bar with a tall Chivas-water the hue of mahogany in front of him. I asked him to return Maria's purse and her ticket to Phoenix, but he only grinned and told me that it was between him and Maria. I said I was going to help her, and he said, "So you're going to take her side?" I said, "Yes, she's right and you're wrong," walked out, and escorted Maria to my car. One can only speculate as to what went through Hunter's mind in the face of such betrayal. An educated guess might be "Right? What the hell does right have to do with anything?" However, Hunter followed me out and shouted, "Good luck getting into the house. It's a fortress, locked up tight as a drum. You'll never get in!"

I drove Maria to Owl Farm, tried the doors and some windows. It was indeed locked tight. She suggested the bathroom window. It's eight feet off the ground, and she hadn't been able to reach it. My own Spider-Man skills weren't up to the task, so I put her on my shoulders and boosted her up, an oddly pleasurable experience. She lifted the window open and climbed in. Drifting through the house, she unlocked the front door for me just as Hunter entered the driveway, his car in a four-wheel drift. He got out and said to me, "Well, that didn't take you long. But good luck finding Maria's stuff. Ho ho!"

Hunter and I watched. In less than a minute Maria appeared with her purse and ticket. With jaw-dropping efficiency she'd gone right to the smoke shelf inside the chimney for her ticket and directly to the freezer for her purse. She knew where her captor hid things. It was an impressive display to me, but painful for Hunter—to be thwarted so easily. We headed to my car as Hunter watched in stunned silence. I drove her to the airport and waited until she boarded her flight.

What to think in the face of such treachery and abandonment? Later, as Hunter watched the sun slide behind the Rocky Mountains, the darkness that fell over Woody Creek was indeed greater than night.

The next evening I called Hunter, and he expressed his admiration for our "defeating" his craft and invited me for a drink, which I accepted, and we watched a basketball game. He knew he had been wrong and never mentioned that day again. I certainly did, when it benefited conversations in the kitchen.

Cleverly Tells Tales of Tex

Edgy Biker, Arctic Racer, and a Fetching Geisha

Tex was a good friend of Hunter's for many years, and they remained buddies until Doc's death. A builder by trade, with a military background, he was known for being able to take care of himself, and would occasionally be called upon when Hunter felt muscle was required. Tex was, and remains, a very private person.

He first met Hunter in San Francisco in 1965. It was 2:00 A.M. and Tex was driving his bike through Golden Gate Park as fast as he possibly could. Just for the fun of it. Suddenly, far ahead, there was a headlight coming at him. Tex eased the bike over to the right. The distant headlight mirrored his move. He eased to the left. Same thing. At that speed, the distance was closing fast.

Every maneuver resulted in the other bike heading straight at him. Tex started to brake. The two bikes missed each other by a few feet.

Tex skidded to a stop, wheeled around, and gave chase. He caught up to Hunter and they came to a halt about twenty yards apart. The men got off. Tex was enraged. Hunter said cheerfully, "I thought I killed you back there!"

Tex pulled his gun. This was a simple case of mistaken identity. A single headlight in the night looks much like the next. Hunter had taken Tex for someone who was at the party he had just left. There was some tension nonetheless. Tex calmed himself and put the piece away. He pulled out a two-gram vial. Hunter had been fairly blasé about the gun, but his eyes widened when he got a load of the cocaine. Tex approached Hunter while unscrewing the cap. When he reached Hunter, he grabbed his hand, turned the vial over and dumped the entire contents out on the back. Doc knew what to do. The men were bonding. Hunter knew of a bar by the water; Tex followed him. They settled onto their barstools, and Tex ordered a shot and a beer. Hunter ordered a Chivas. Tex took a look at Hunter's drink, swept his own off the bar, and ordered three double Chivases apiece. It was the beginning of their friendship.

A snowy winter night in 1976, it was the heyday of the J-Bar. Eleven o'clock, prime time, and the bar was full. Outside, the snow, blowing sideways, had accumulated and drifted. The entire town, including Main Street, was covered by at least a foot of the stuff. Inside, Tex and Hunter were part of the mix. It being the seventies, we'll never know exactly how many of the revelers were on acid that night, but we can be sure of two. Tex and Hunter had dropped two hits each, and it was taking hold quite nicely, thank you. Their conversation had turned to their respective driving skills. Hunter always fancied himself an ace driver, and Tex was of the same opinion regarding his own talents. Fact was, they were both absolutely sure that, given the opportunity, each could drive the other into oblivion. A challenge was inevitable. The twelve inches of unplowed snow on the roads wasn't a factor.

Hunter had "the Shark," a 1972 Chevy Caprice, fire-engine red 454 convertible, directly out front in a convenient No Parking zone. Tex was piloting a metallic gray Coupe de Ville. It was parked, more or less legally, just across the street. After some conversation regarding the relative merits of the vehicles, it was decided that a fair handicap would be to race in reverse, culminating with a 180-degree turn and a parallel park in front of the J-Bar. The race would begin at the Hickory House restaurant a mile down Main Street. The judges were then-sheriff Dick Kienast, and Michael Solheim, who ran the J-Bar. There was no traffic.

Courtesy of Deborah Fuller

Hunter and *Rolling Stone* editor Tobias Perse in "the Shark": an all-weather racer.

Courtesy of Deborah Fuller

"The Shark," grazing in a field beside the Tavern with Woody Creek writer Gaylord Guenin.

So much snow had accumulated that it took several large men to push the behemoths out of their parking spaces. Once in the street, they were ready to go. For some reason no one wanted to accompany the guys to the Hickory House to be the official starter. It would have meant walking all the way back to the Jerome in a blizzard, or riding with one of them. Neither option seemed prudent to even the most loaded of those assembled. A crowd gathered on the sidewalk and watched the two monstrous vehicles disappear like spirits into the storm. As snow began to accumulate on the windward side of their faces, people glanced around at one another. Why were they standing there in the snow? All but a few slipped back into the bar. Those who stayed out on the sidewalk were tourists not wanting to take the chance of missing Hunter Thompson racing in reverse in a blizzard. The locals, warm and drinking inside, knew that they'd get the word when something actually happened.

It wasn't long before one of the tourists, covered with an inch of fresh powder, came charging into the bar. "I think they're coming!" Everyone headed out to the sidewalk. In the vague distance, taillights and back-up lights appeared. Reverse racing is exciting in its own way, but not in the sense of high speeds. Even if you are willing to blow an engine, the reverse-gear ratio is such that truly dangerous speeds aren't possible. The crowd hadn't missed much between the announcement and actually getting out to the sidewalk. The contestants were still just barely coming into view. Steering is the true challenge in reverse. Especially through twelve inches of snow. Total concentration is required. One too-abrupt crank of the wheel and you're doing 360s until all your momentum is dissipated. Through the driving snow the lights slowly grew larger, holding steady, not swerving. It was the whine of the engines that was painful, revving so far beyond the red line, tortured beyond reason. The Jerome was the finish, and the No Parking spaces directly in front were the destination.

The great Red Shark was ahead by a length and a half when the racers became clearly visible. The crowd could hear Tex's de Ville winding down, but Hunter maintained speed. He spun the Shark around and braked—to no avail. The inertia of the huge machine was too much. The Shark glided past the Jerome and through the intersection beyond without slowing—up over the curb and through the wrought-iron fence that surrounded the lawn of a small restaurant, coming to a rest on its doorstep. In the meantime, Tex had executed a perfect spin and slid up next to the curb in a textbook example of parallel parking. He was declared winner without protest, by everyone but Hunter. Hunter insisted that getting there first had made him the winner, even though he got "there" and then some. Never mind the parking job on the lawn of the restaurant. Naturally Tex ended up buying the drinks anyway.

———

Halloween was usually pretty interesting in Aspen. It was 1984 and Hunter was sitting alone in the kitchen at Owl Farm. There was a knock on the door. Hunter opened it to find three geishas standing there. Not an everyday occurrence, at Owl Farm or anyplace else in Woody Creek. Always good with the composure, Hunter graciously invited them inside.

The week before, Tex had been remodeling a space to accommodate Aspen's next sushi bar. He had been befriended by Masa, the owner, and the other Japanese who were constantly coming and going. They were excited about Halloween; relatively new in town, they had heard the wild stories. On the day of Halloween, one of them asked Tex if he was going to dress up that evening. When the large, somewhat violent biker announced that he was planning on going as a geisha this year, his new Japanese friends were enthusiastic. Later that afternoon they showed up with a homemade geisha wig attached to a baseball cap with the bill cut off. This was great. The wig was going to be the hard part. The rest of the outfit—kimono, etc.—fell into place with no problem.

That evening Tex found himself at a very high-tone party in Aspen's exclusive Starwood subdivision. Remarkably, unbelievably, there were two beautiful Asian girls there, dressed as geishas. Maybe they actually were geishas; we'll never know. Tex was not a shy man anyway, but what an ice-breaker. There he stood, full geisha attire, white pancake makeup, the works, chatting up these two beautiful women. Tex didn't let the fact that they described their function at the party as "entertainment" keep him from suggesting that they split and go meet the famous author. I guess they didn't take their jobs too seriously, because they thought the idea was just dandy, and off the three went to Owl Farm.

When they arrived, Tex didn't identify himself and maintained almost complete silence. Hunter was particularly enchanted by the tall, quiet geisha. She said almost nothing, but partook of the hospitality of the Owl Farm kitchen just as eagerly as the two smaller ones. As the evening unfolded, a mixture of substances did their work on the inhibitions in the room, and Hunter felt that a special, exotic sort of love was in the air. Tex was becoming a little uncomfortable with all the options that might present themselves to him if he stayed. Coming clean with Hunter and a houseful of weapons definitely wasn't one of them. Showing true wisdom, Tex slipped out into the night, leaving the two girls there.

No one will tell the story of how Hunter found out the truth, but from that night on, Tex's name at Owl Farm was the Princess of Darkness.

Documentary filmmaker Wayne Ewing chronicled Hunter Thompson's adventures for twenty years. His efforts produced a trilogy of films, *Breakfast With Hunter*, *When I Die*, and *Free Lisl: Fear and Loathing in Denver*. Hunter and Wayne's relationship was much more than professional: they were close friends and, occasionally through the years, neighbors. Wayne was often described as possibly the most decent man to frequent the kitchen. It was Hunter's kitchen; the bar wasn't too high. Being Hunter's friend was an ongoing learning experience; the early lessons were often the most exciting.

Hunter had decided that he needed a new camera. Wayne, being a professional cameraman, got discounts and was glad to order whatever Hunter needed. The camera arrived, and Wayne called Doc to see if he wanted to take delivery. Hunter told Wayne to come right over. "Just walk in and make yourself at home. I might be in the shower." Wayne was puzzled. Why not just wait until Hunter was out of the shower? Go over in a little while. Not wanting to argue unnecessarily, Wayne and his girlfriend headed out for Owl Farm. They arrived and knocked for a fair amount of time. After a while Wayne tried the door; it was unlocked.

Well, okay. Hunter had said come on in; Wayne was uneasy. He told his girlfriend to wait as he gingerly pushed the door open and stepped inside. "Hunter! Hunter, it's Wayne . . . I've come with the camera." No response. Then, perhaps, a small sound from the next room. Wayne crept through the living room toward the kitchen. "Hunter, it's Wayne. I'm here."

Standing in the kitchen doorway, he observed Hunter in the middle of the room—in his bathrobe and dripping wet. The only thing to suggest that he wasn't just out of the shower was the sawed-off twelve-gauge in his hand hanging by his side and a maniacal grin on his face. "My god," Wayne thought, "he can shoot me dead and claim he thought I was an intruder." Hunter fired from the hip. The blast tore a four-inch hole in the doorframe, twelve inches from Wayne's thigh. Wayne bolted for the porch, grabbed the girlfriend, and ran for the car. Hunter gave chase.

When Doc caught up with the unnerved couple he was laughing. He persuaded them to come back. Wayne had just learned that this was just one of Hunter's many unique ways of giving you a little hug. He also learned that you really could get hurt.

When asked what he gleaned from all his years with Hunter, Wayne paused as if he'd never given it any thought before, after a moment he said, "Hunter taught me how to gamble, how to be a good gambler." You bet. It was always a gamble.

Wayne pointed out that on the rare occasion when Hunter would have to write a check to pay off his kitchen gambling debts, he would always write "bad gambling debt" in the memo portion of the check, in the hope that the check would end up framed on a wall rather than be cashed. It often worked.

Over the course of the years of trailing after Hunter, documenting his antics, Wayne evolved into a de facto road manager. When Hunter was invited to Washington to participate in George McGovern's eightieth birthday celebration, Wayne was the obvious choice to be Hunter's advance man. He was from D.C. and knew his way around as a local.

On the day of Hunter's arrival, Wayne was supposed to rent a limousine, pick Hunter up at Dulles airport, and get him checked into his hotel suite. Hunter's plane touched down, and Wayne waited at the gate. And waited, and waited. Wayne waited so long that he figured there couldn't possibly be anyone left on the plane. He concluded that Hunter had missed the flight, and he was about to leave when Hunter appeared. He was like a rubber man. His legs weren't supporting him and he was groping from handhold to handhold. "I need a wheelchair" was Hunter's greeting to Wayne. No shit. Wayne looked around and, amazingly, there sat a wheelchair, as if they had ordered it. Wayne poured Hunter into it. As they wheeled their way toward the limo, Wayne was thinking that, yes, there was surely an interesting explanation but, no, he would probably never hear it. Hunter proceeded to explain.

Boarding the plane in Denver, Hunter almost immediately got into an argument with the stewardess. Clearly the woman had no idea that she was talking to someone to whom the usual rules did not apply. Hunter found this offensive. Apparently there was a thing or two about his behavior that the stewardess found offensive. One rule that she must have been unaware of, in regard to Hunter, was that you don't fight back. Things got ugly. Hunter, in a breathtaking moment of insight, decided that things could get worse. He went to his seat and took a halcyon, or two, or . . . His reasoning was that if he were unconscious, the problems would diminish. Unfortunately, the sleeping pills lasted longer than the flight.

The limousine wove through D.C. traffic and reached the hotel forty-five minutes later. Sans wheelchair, Wayne escorted Hunter to the hotel bar and left him. At the front desk, Wayne checked "Ben Franklin" into a suite. Then he returned to the lounge to fetch Hunter. The whole process had taken about five minutes, and in that time Hunter had not only regained his composure but was in the process of successfully picking up a woman. An exceptionally attractive, straight-laced lady lawyer from Memphis was saying, "Aren't you that . . . uh . . . writer?"

Back in Colorado, back in the kitchen, Wayne and some of the boys were waiting for the game to start. We were also waiting for Hunter to come out of the bedroom. We were always excited about the beginning of a new football season, but it was hell on Hunter's schedule. The early game would start at eleven o'clock Mountain Time, sleepy time for Doc. It was, in fact, hours and hours earlier than his usual wake-up call. So the first few games of football season involved a fair amount of waiting. We'd set ourselves up in the kitchen, and Deborah or Anita would begin the process of getting him up and running.

On this particular occasion, we were passing the time talking about the kind of expectations people have of Hunter. We'd all seen it: an outsider would come into the kitchen hoping to find some kind of crazed caricature, only to encounter a sedate middle-aged man in thoughtful conversation. A student attending a lecture by the world-famous author would end up watching people getting blasted with a fire extinguisher. Wayne told us about an incident in a very fancy London restaurant.

Hunter was in England on business, having meetings with his overseas publisher. The publisher was wining and dining him at all the best places. This particular evening they were at a posh joint with the oak paneling and the very proper East Indian staff. The publisher was obviously well known there, and it was clear that they were expecting the great writer from the States. While they were enjoying their meal, an American couple seated on the other side of the room spotted Hunter and the publisher. The couple recognized Hunter and were big fans. They sent a note over by way of the Indian maître d', whose exotic accent and perfect diction probably intimidated everyone but the queen. The note was lovely and gracious, indicating that they didn't wish to interrupt his meal but wanted Hunter to know that they were fellow Americans, and what high regard they held him in. What might these folks' expectations have been?

Hunter read the note, paused for a bit, then affected a look of utter horror and outrage. He beckoned wildly for the maître d' to come to the table. The Indian arrived, all formality and propriety. Hunter had him lean low over the table so he could whisper in his ear. Hunter whispered, and the maître d' straightened instantly. He glared at the American couple across the room. The Indian motioned at minions as he strode briskly toward the American couple. When he arrived at their table, his body language and gestures were intimidating even from ten yards away. He put his hand on the man's shoulder as if to physically pick him up out of his chair. The woman rose as waiters rushed toward them with their coats. The maître d' ushered them to the front of the restaurant with a hand on each of their elbows. When they arrived at the door, he finally raised his voice. "And never return to this establishment," he declared in his perfect diction and accent.

Hunter had told the Indian that the couple had been trying to sell him drugs.

On football game days the boys waited in the kitchen. There was no rule about not going into Hunter's bedroom, but there was no reason to; Deborah was already in there. Sometimes Doc would just disappear, and after a while you'd have to go check to see if he was ever coming out. You might find him fast asleep or just needing some quiet time. There were some rules, however. Most of them weren't written down, but some were. NEVER DIAL 911, handwritten and taped to the refrigerator. FRIENDS OF FRIENDS CAN'T BRING FRIENDS, printed on a little sign. Hunter was very serious about the former, not as worried about the latter. There was also a sign in the bathroom, on the toilet, indicating the sorts of things that weren't supposed to be thrown in there. It was a sensitive, high-tech toilet. Then there were the rules that weren't written down anywhere but that you might be informed of. There were also unspoken rules.

One spoken, and generally accepted as good sense, rule was that if you brought someone into the kitchen, you were responsible for that person. The consequences for not tending to a guest who might have gotten caught up in the moment, or possibly ingested something that didn't agree with him, could be unpleasant indeed. An example of the very worst kind of guest one might bring by the kitchen would be litigious women. Hunter really hated it when someone invaded his space and then sued him. Unbelievably, this sort of thing happened. It led to the "Never encroach on Hunter's physical space" rule. He actually had next to his chair one of those red velvet ropes that keep people like Cleverly out of trendy nightclubs. And there were occasions when he had to use it. The thing about getting into Hunter's space behind the counter was that he had countless weapons within arm's reach. Getting too close could be dangerous.

On one occasion I brought my landlady to a crowded play-off game. Hunter was glad to have her; she was a neighbor, a major landowner, and something of a legend in the community. We said hello to Hunter, and she immediately took up position directly behind him. I couldn't stand it. I kept waiting for him to lash out with a cattle prod or a dagger. She stayed there for the whole first quarter. When she finally moved off to the buffet in the living room, I thanked Hunter for not doing her in. She was the best landlady I ever had, and I didn't want to lose her.

Another practical rule was to never make reference to an HST quote in front of Hunter if you couldn't instantly put your hands on it. Most of Doc's books were right there, and you had better at least know which book to look in. Chapter and page was the only way to be totally safe. Hunter needed to be quoted accurately and would almost certainly want the whole shooting match read aloud. Being less than completely informed could be dangerous.

If watching a game, which the boys were about to do, it was a good idea to not discuss anything but the game during the game. You could find yourself sitting next to the most interesting person in the world, but what started out as a whispered aside could evolve into an engrossing conversation and could eventually catch the attention of Hunter, and unpleasantness could ensue.

It was an extremely good idea not to interject when Hunter was talking to an attractive woman. It was a good idea not to get between Hunter and an attractive woman. It was a good idea not to get anywhere near the view plane that existed between Hunter and an attractive woman. Should any of this occur, it was a good idea to remember the rule about not fighting back.

Braudis Explains the Birth of Shotgun Golf

If Thomas Edison had not invented the lightbulb, someone else would have gotten around to it eventually. The same goes for many of our finest inventions. But only Hunter could have invented shotgun golf. Only Hunter, with the physique and hand-eye coordination of a natural athlete, would have found the similarities between golf and skeet shooting so obvious. There were many things about Hunter that the country club golfing crowd didn't approve of, but the sight of the butt of a twelve-gauge sticking out of his golf bag filled them with a kind of unease they could scarcely comprehend.

It was midsummer in the late eighties. Hunter had received a set of Ping beryllium golf clubs, hand-me-downs from his brother. A few years earlier these clubs had been considered a breakthrough in sports technology. Made from a hard metallic element commonly used in atomic reactors, the irons were widely believed to enhance the scores of the weekend golfer. Hunter had never swung them.

Hunter had created a one-hole golf course in the meadow at Owl Farm that doubled as a firearms range. The "green" was a twelve-by-twelve square of linoleum salvaged from one of his domestic remodels and placed on the grass about a hundred yards from the house. The pin was a unfurled beach umbrella stabbed through the center of the linoleum and into the soft earth. The "pin" provided a target and a crude range finder. The golf clubs were still in their bag and secured by a blanket that had been duct-taped over the club heads, forming an improvised traveling bag for the clubs. This same bag had flown from Aspen to Phoenix the winter before for the previously mentioned and aborted golf vacation, when Hunter was officially on assignment for the *San Francisco Examiner* to cover the impeachment hearings for Evan Mecham.

Back in Woody Creek, I stripped the duct tape and blanket from the golf bag and pulled out the nine iron and pitching wedge. At Hunter's request, I had brought a couple hundred used golf balls. Hunter started swinging at balls in order the hit the "green." None of his shots came close.Frustrated, he asked me to try. After flying balls over the linoleum with the nine iron, I picked up the wedge and "Plop," my first shot landed audibly on the square. I repeated the lofting shots a few times with persistent accuracy.

Hunter tried a few shots with the wedge and got more frustrated. He was stiff and rusty. Modern golf technology couldn't help his swing. Unwilling to waste a beautiful summer afternoon, Hunter suggested that I hit the high wedges while he tried to shoot them in mid-flight with a double-barreled side-by-side twelve-gauge shotgun.

We arranged his firing position to pose no danger to the golfer or the yuppie mountain bikers from Arkansas, as he referred to them, pedaling along the road past Owl Farm.

I would pop a high arching ball toward the pin, and Hunter would shoot. After six or seven attempts to hit the ball, and with no obvious deviation in its flight, Hunter replaced the light 7 1/2 shot with a heavier and larger number-four shot. The results didn't change.

Hunter was nearing that level of disappointment that I recognized as the onset of a temper tantrum, which would lead me to go home while his temper continued into his future activities that evening, so I suggested that the mass of the ball, its surface,

Courtesy of Dan Dibble

Hunter with his favorite club in the bag . . . twelve-gauge.

speed, size, and trajectory, might have something to do with the appearance that Hunter's aim could be in the same category as his golf swing. My proposed experiment involved somehow suspending a golf ball in the air and having Hunter shoot at it from a distance similar to the range between him and the earlier balls while they were in flight.

Hunter went into the house and came out with a roll of cellophane tape and a peacock plume. He taped a golf ball to one end of the plume and taped the other end of the plume to a willow bush. Standing about twenty yards from the target, he loaded the shotgun, aimed, and fired. No movement of the golf ball. He raised the weapon, took aim, fired, and got the same results. We approached the ball and found evidence of lead transfer on the white jacket of the Titlist.

Our conclusion was that the triggerman may have been hitting the moving targets but did not have any effect on the balls' flight path. "Hot damn!" shouted HST.

Shotgun golf died a natural death. It was reincarnated about twenty-five years later in Hunter's column at ESPN.com. His new version was replete with rules, and of course the match could be wagered on. It was reprinted in Hunter's book *Hey, Rube*. I doubt anyone else will attempt a match outside their imaginations.

Courtesy of Sara Diamond

A potential caddy at the *Hey, Rube* book signing that Walter Issacson threw at the Aspen Institute.

Hunter Goes to War, and Doesn't Much Care for It

Loren Jenkins was one of Hunter's friends from his earliest days in Aspen. Jenkins was Saigon bureau chief for *Newsweek* magazine during the Vietnam War, and later was Rome bureau chief for the *Washington Post*. He won a Pulitzer Prize for his work in Lebanon and is now senior foreign editor for National Public Radio. He and his wife, Missie Thorne, now live in D.C. but maintain a home in Old Snowmass, just down the road from Aspen. When in town, Loren was a fixture in the kitchen, being good friends with all the regulars, including Ed Bradley, whom he was close to in Vietnam. Loren was the first person Hunter called when *Rolling Stone* sent him to 'Nam, and the two hooked up again when they covered the U.S. invasion of Grenada.

Prior to their move to Old Snowmass, Loren and Missie lived on McLain Flats Road. McLain Flats is the back way to Woody Creek from Aspen. Sometimes, returning from town late at night, it was a good idea to take the back way. If one suspected the headlights in the rearview mirror of belonging to a peace officer, one could pop in and pay Loren and Missie a visit. Hunter was an occasional visitor.

Hunter's drop-ins would usually be the product of paranoia, and would always be very late, after the bars closed. Loren and Missie found this more amusing than annoying. Hunter would barge in whether they were in bed or awake, and the three of them would sit around and shoot the shit until Hunter thought the "danger" had passed. Occasionally Hunter's hosts would be out for the evening. This wouldn't deter him; he'd still have to hide out till the "heat was off," so he'd let himself in and occupy himself by relocating small household objects. When Loren and Missie returned home, they'd be vaguely disorientated: things wouldn't be quite the same, and eventually they'd decide that Hunter had been there. When Loren and Missie moved to Old Snowmass, a few miles down valley, they sold the McLain Flats house to a young professional couple. The couple was just starting a family; both were attorneys. But the fact that Hunter's friends no longer lived there, that the house had changed hands, didn't deter him at all. The new owners would find him hanging out in their living room, lying low, at all hours. Jenkins explained that Doc went with the house.

'NAM: HUNTER ARRIVES

In January 1975, Vietnam began to come apart. Loren Jenkins was in Nepal working for *Newsweek*. When the shit hit the fan, he was transferred to Saigon. On April 28, 1975, Saigon fell, and it was over. When things went south, they went south fast.

In early February of that year the provincial capital Boun Me Thuot was overrun, and at that point it was clear to all that the end was near. A month later Hunter called Loren and said he had a job covering the war and wanted to know what it was like over there. Loren illuminated him: "It was what it was, the end of a war." Hoping for some more useful details, Hunter then called Loren's first wife, Nancy, who was in Hong Kong. After a lengthy conversation, he concluded that it was what it was.

In late March, Hunter flew from Aspen to Hong Kong. He allowed himself three days in Hong Kong to buy "equipment" before heading to Saigon. During that time, Loren called him and asked that he stop by the *Newsweek* bureau and pick up some cash. Loren had a staff of fifteen: five Western correspondents and the rest locals. They had to be paid, and there were operating expenses. No one was taking checks at that point. Loren wanted Hunter to grab forty thousand dollars in cash. He said, "Don't put it in your bag. You have to tape it to your body."

When Hunter got off the plane in Saigon he was perspiring heavily. The shock of the tropical heat after the air-conditioned airplane messed with his chemistry. He was dressed exactly like Hunter S. Thompson: Aloha shirt, Bermudas, tennis sneakers. While this was acceptable vacation wear back in the States, it wasn't exactly normal in Saigon at the end of an ugly war. It was also terrible camouflage for someone smuggling forty thousand dollars in U.S. currency. Hunter spotted a sign declaring ANYONE CARRYING OVER $100 IN CASH WILL FACE PROSECUTION. This produced an entirely different kind of sweat. Hunter was sure that he could smell the difference, and that everyone else could, too. Even the finest duct tape wasn't designed to hold up against this sort of nervous perspiration. He became displeased with his friend Loren Jenkins. He became edgy. But he persevered.

There were two hotels in Saigon preferred by the foreign press, the Caravel, a slick modern edifice where the TV types stayed, and the Continental Palace, a fine old colonial building, the hotel of Graham Greene, where the print journalists holed up. When Loren returned to the Palace that afternoon the manager rushed up to him. "There was an American here looking for you. . . . I think he's CIA." Loren asked what made him think that. The manager's reply suggested that the fellow's odd dress and strange behavior could only be explained as that of an inept American spy. "He wanted a room. I told him we had none. I can find him one if you like." Loren told the manager that he was pretty sure he knew who the gentleman was, that he wasn't a spy, and that, yes, he should be given a room. He then headed to the bar. Shortly thereafter he was confronting a fairly agitated Hunter Thompson. "I've been ripped off." Loren felt dizzy, assuming the worst. "My forty thousand!"

After being turned away from the Continental Palace, Hunter's keen instincts had somehow led him straight to Tu Do Street, the center of sin and vice in Saigon. The district was clogged with prostitutes, beggars, and grifters of every shape and form. There was a thriving black-market business exchanging U.S. dollars for piastras. There was also a common scam involving that business.

The black marketeer would offer the "mark" a good exchange rate, usually on a hundred dollars, and as he was handing the gringo a roll of Vietnamese currency, he would look over the mark's shoulder and say the Saigon equivalent of "Cheese it, the cops! Split up. You go that way!" The two would take off in opposite directions, and when the mark stopped running and stepped into a bar or restaurant to count his money he'd find one small denomination note wrapped around a roll of paper. This is what had happened to Hunter. Loren was profoundly relieved: a hundred dollars of Hunter's own money was an acceptable loss.

Loren's relief was short-lived, as Hunter immediately launched into a rant about the awkwardness at the airport, which he perceived as a setup and betrayal. In a brilliant flanking action, Loren interrupted and mentioned that he'd procured a room for Hunter, but that the manager thought he was with the CIA. This insult bored directly into Hunter's dark heart, and as he started sputtering about the great pride he felt at being on Richard Nixon's enemies list, the little "thing" at the airport was instantly forgotten. There had been no incident at customs anyway. Hunter felt that his press credentials had gotten him through; Loren secretly thought that the authorities probably figured that no real smuggler would ever be that obvious.

Loren got Hunter checked into a room and they agreed to meet an hour later. The Continental Palace had a lovely courtyard, bar, and restaurant on the ground floor. Because of the 9:00 P.M. curfew in Saigon, this was where the press corps spent their evenings. The journalists would file their stories from their rooms, do whatever they had to do on the streets, and be back in the bar by nine. Hunter and Loren met in the courtyard, and Loren introduced Hunter around to the assembled press, about half of whom were pretty excited to meet him.

There was also a Mr. Chu, well known at the hotel but not a member of the press corps. Mr. Chu and his Samsonite case would turn up at the hotel sometime around the dinner hour. Several journalists, Chu, and the case would often retire to one of the reporters' rooms. In the case were pipes, lamps, and opium. Opium was the drug of choice in Southeast Asia. Graham Greene favored it. A subtle, old-school drug, opium is usually associated with peaceful ruminating, a clear head, and perfect recall the following day. Hunter Thompson was invited upstairs with the fellas. Later Loren Jenkins was told that Hunter had two or three pipes, a large dose.

The gang returned downstairs, and Loren joined them for dinner. It was a fairly large group. Well into the meal, Hunter excused himself and headed to the men's room. The doors to the bathrooms were separated from the dining room by only a large bamboo screen, which Hunter disappeared behind. Minutes later blood-curdling screams were heard coming from that direction. Every head in the dining room snapped around. "LOREN, LOREN, HELP!"

As Loren sprang to his feet, Hunter came crashing through the screen, sprawling onto the dining room floor. He was hyperventilating, panicked; they almost called a doctor. Hunter's drug Achilles' heel had been discovered. The next day he admitted to Jenkins that he had actually done opium once before, with the same effect. You'd think he would have remembered that beforehand.

'NAM: SAIGON FALLS

The North Vietnamese Army was pushing south. Quang Tri fell, then Hue. The conversation in the courtyard of the Continental Palace centered on what the journalists would do when the North Vietnamese got to Saigon. Bug out? Stay and report? Stay and fight? There were many loony scenarios. Some of the macho types thought they should arm themselves. Jenkins and the old hands felt this was a lousy idea; their neutrality was their only real defense. The gung ho cowboys were asked to find a new place to live.

At this point Hunter had been in Saigon for four or five days, and he announced that he was going to Hong Kong. Loren was incredulous: "You're here to write *Fear and Loathing in Saigon*, not Hong Kong." Loren was deeply disappointed, Saigon was as crazy as a place can get, and being a great admirer of Hunter's writing, he truly felt that Doc was the perfect person to report it. Hunter insisted that the trip was absolutely necessary, claiming that *Rolling Stone* editor Jann Wenner had canceled his insurance before he had left the States and that he had to get that situation cleared up before he faced any more unreasonable danger. Once again Loren was incredulous. It seemed that Hunter only liked danger when he was the most dangerous person in the room. The situation in Saigon was far beyond Hunter's, or anyone's, control; it was an entirely different sort of danger. In any case, Hunter spent six days in Hong Kong and then returned to Saigon. Loren was pleased to see him but mildly concerned about the huge footlocker he was traveling with. Anything could be in it.

It turned out that Hunter had decided to organize the press corps. The footlocker was full of high-tech equipment: tape recorders, walkie-talkies and all manner of sneaky electronic devices. He wanted to wire everyone; there were code words and passwords. The international press corps, jaded war correspondents, were about as cynical as you could get. They had no idea what to make of Doc's efforts.

All this time, he hadn't written a word. Since this certainly wasn't Hunter's first rodeo, he knew how to hedge his bets, so he had a large top-of-the-line reel-to-reel tape recorder and was recording everything as events unfolded, in case he ever did decide to write. When Loren got a 3:00 A.M. phone call from the New York office (post three-martini lunch, New York time), Hunter was there recording. When Loren patiently explained that, no, he couldn't get a photo of the presidential palace with a tank in front of it and a hot chick standing in front of the tank, because there were no tanks or hot chicks in front of the palace, and because he didn't stage photographs, Hunter got it. When Hunter was out in the field listening to a speech given by an American colonel to his troops indicating that they were going to fight to the last man, Hunter got the speech—and, in the background, the sound of a chopper as it approached, landed, and swept the colonel off to safety. This was good stuff.

One week before the fall of Saigon, Hunter announced, "I gotta fly to Laos." Loren, again, couldn't believe it. This was it, the big show, surely the most significant event in Hunter's journalistic career. Saigon was where the story was. Hunter was adamant. "I have to watch this thing from Laos." He flew to the sleepy town of Ban Dien and stayed there as Saigon fell. As near as Jenkins can remember, the only writing Hunter ever published on the fall of Saigon was a cable he shot off to Jann Wenner bitching about the insurance situation and asking for more expense money.

The night before Hunter left for Laos, he and Loren were chatting about what would happen next. The only "next" that Loren was interested in was his own, not Vietnam's. He told Hunter about a little thatched hotel on a beach on the island of Bali. That was his "next."

Loren had told the American ambassador to Vietnam that he wasn't leaving the country until the ambassador did, so he was on one of the last choppers out of the embassy compound. From there, he flew to an aircraft carrier, where he spent four days as it steamed to Subic Bay. During his time at sea he filed his final dispatches on the fall of Saigon and the end of the United States' Vietnam adventure. Loren's editors told him to take as much time off as he wanted, and he soon

Courtesy of Loren Jenkins

Loren Jenkins on the roof of the U.S. Embassy in Saigon, waiting to be flown to the carrier.

found himself in a bungalow on the beach at the hotel Tan Jun Sari on Bali.

The decompression process after months of covering combat is a difficult one. Sleep doesn't come easily, one remains wired, the blades on the overhead fan are the rotors of a gunship, unexpected sounds suggest danger. On his second morning on Bali, Loren was startled awake at 4:00 A.M. to the sounds of battle. Was it in his head? No, it was in the room. There was Hunter, standing by the door with one of his high-tech tape recorders playing, at full volume, the war in Vietnam. Loren was less than amused. Hunter thought it was funny as hell.

Hunter had flown to Bali with a beautiful blonde. In the blonde's makeup case was a jar of face powder. Not really. The jar was full of organic mescaline; the two look much the same. The three of them spent the next week on the beach consuming it. Hunter had missed the battle but made it to the after party.

Courtesy of Laura Thorne

Hunter and Loren, more than a few years after their adventures at war.

GRENADA: THE GREAT WRITER, THE HAND, AND THE FIGHT

Loren Jenkins was the only journalist to bring a date to the invasion of Grenada. In October of 1983 he was working for the *Washington Post*. When the United States invaded Grenada, the *Post* sent Loren to Barbados, which was the closest you could get to the island after the initial wave of Marines moved in. The navy kept the press away for four days after the invasion, and then would fly in groups on C130s for three or four hours at a time.

The invasion followed the bombing of the Marine barracks in Beirut. The soldiers who invaded Grenada had been heading for Lebanon and were diverted to the island. Loren thought the whole thing was a face-saving move to secure a victory after the tragic loss of 241 lives to Hezbollah terrorists.

Still, on October 13 there had been a bloody coup on the island led by Marxist Barnard Coard, who then installed himself as dep-

Courtesy of Loren Jenkins

Loren Jenkins at the Floridita Bar in Havana, drinking with a statue of Ernest Hemingway—which is not at all like drinking with Hunter, Braudis, and Cleverly.

uty prime minister, with crony Maurice Bishop as prime minister. This didn't sit well with the Reagan administration, or jibe with its war on communism. When improvements were started on the Grenada airport, the administration decided that the airport was being brought up to military grade, that the Grenadan government wasn't just trying to improve tourist capacity. There was a Cuban military presence on the island, and some engineers, not to mention a thousand U.S. medical students. That was good enough for us.

The result was operation "Urgent Fury." Twelve hundred Marines stormed the island and initially met with heavy resistance. By the time our force reached seven thousand, the resistance had dissolved, and whatever fighters were left were fleeing into the mountains. When the press corps was finally allowed to occupy the island, most stayed at the St. George Hotel in the capital. When Loren realized that he'd probably be there for three or four weeks, he called Missie and urged her to join him; the water was fine. Hunter got wind of the fun to be had and convinced *Rolling Stone* that this was an assignment custom-made for you know who. He left for the island a day before Missie, and arrived two days after she did. Where Hunter's missing three days went, he wouldn't say.

A few days later, Loren encountered the great writer V. S. Naipaul, who had just checked into the St. George. When Loren next saw Hunter, he told him that "he wasn't the most famous writer in the hotel anymore, that V. S. Naipaul was staying there." Hunter replied, "Who's V. S. Naipaul?" Later Hunter and Naipaul met and became great friends. Before long, the press corps tired of the St. George and its location in the middle of the capital city, so they, en masse, liberated a small beachfront hotel called Hidden Bay. There they spent their days swimming, drinking, and attending briefings at which the military would try to convince them that they were busy hunting down commies in the mountains.

One day Hunter, Loren, and Missie were driving through a village, and one of them looked down an alley and noticed a garbage can with a human hand sticking out of it. Hunter insisted they stop. With Missie snapping pictures, the guys cautiously approached, as if the thing could become aware. There was a khaki sleeve on its arm. As they closed in on the gruesome tableau, they realized that the hand was a prosthetic. This was even better, and Hunter grabbed the prize. The thing wasn't just an inanimate lump of plastic; it was articulated. By manipulating the end where it would have attached to the stump, he could make the fingers move in an eerie, lifelike manner. Hunter couldn't believe his good fortune.

The next few days saw a lot of the kind of pranks that are really funny if they're not being played on you. Waiters and waitresses, bartenders, people driving cars with Hunter in the backseat, and random victims on the street all met "the hand," with its grasping, twitching fingers. Hunter created an elaborate mythology surrounding the discovery of the hand, which of course bore little or no relation to actual events. It became an instant legend among the press corps. Unlike its previous owner, Hunter and the hand were inseparable.

Hunter was determined to bring the thing back to the States with him. There was Woody Creek, and worlds far beyond Woody Creek, for him and the hand to conquer. Sadly for Hunter, there was a physician present during one of his performances. He took an immediate interest in the hand and explained how really sophisticated and expensive the thing was. In other words, it wasn't a toy. Says who? For Hunter this was a really crummy turn of events. The hand was the best toy he'd come upon in ages. The doctor was adamant, though. The thing had to belong to someone out there who, undoubtedly, would be missing it badly once he sobered up. If not, someone else could make real use of it. Hunter was of the strong opinion that *he* was making real use of it, but it was hard not to listen to reason. With great reluctance, he relinquished his prize. What followed was a period of mourning for him, and perhaps to some degree for Missie and Loren as well. The rest of the island fell into two categories, past victims of the hand and future victims of the hand. Had they known about Hunter's loss, I suspect they would have had different feelings on the matter.

The three thought that a trip into the mountains would cheer them up. There was a fine restaurant called Mama's that was reputed to serve an excellent conch soup. They set out in an open Jeep. About halfway to their destination, after several miles of rough roads and switchbacks, they came to a sudden halt. The road was blocked by U.S. troops. It was a checkpoint to keep the phantom Cuban army from sneaking around the island.

Deb Fuller and Bob at the Jenkins wedding.

Instead of being waved on through as they fully expected, the three were detained. The hood of the jeep was raised and a thorough inspection of the vehicle was begun. Loren Jenkins was displeased. He had endured this sort of thing in countless Third World war zones at the hands of petty military types, and he wasn't happy to have to take this sort of crap from our own guys. He and Hunter produced their press credentials, with little effect. Jesus Christ, this was the world-famous Hunter S. Thompson. This was Loren Jenkins. You know, with the Pulitzer Prize. This was a beautiful blonde who couldn't be more an American WASP and less a Cuban spy if she had USA tattooed on her forehead.

Loren's patience stretched and then snapped. He launched into a tirade. "What the hell are you people doing here, anyway?" He went on to suggest that our government would be better off minding its own business, and from there he went on to vent his

Loren Jenkins and Missie Thorne's wedding. The beautiful Barbara Groh with Benton, Cleverly, and Braudis, who come in assorted sizes.

spleen at large, expressing political leanings somewhat to the left of Fidel and Mao. The young soldiers felt pretty sure that people without guns probably should be civil to people with guns. They put Loren facedown on the ground and cuffed his hands behind his back. This was too much. Missie was the next to snap. She yanked off her sandal and proceeded to use it to beat one of the soldiers on the helmet, all the while Loren keeping up his rant from the dirt.

Hunter's pain over the loss of the hand was instantly replaced with the bliss of chaos. This is what he lived for. The scene continued for some minutes, with Hunter cheering everyone on just to keep the action going. An officer finally showed up and witnessed, with mouth agape, his boys bullying the very press corps that they had spent so much time sucking up to. The officer had Loren released immediately, and no one was sorry to see the group head up the road toward the restaurant. The conch soup was just as good as they had been told.

Grenada was our first war with Cuba, and our first military victory since long before Vietnam. It was also the first time since before World War II that a communist government had been replaced with a pro-Western one. Being the fierce patriot, Hunter must have been very proud.

Hunter's Friend Dabbles in the Business and Pays the Price

Ed Hoban—University of Notre Dame, class of 1972, Lompoc Federal Prison, class of 1984—was a close friend of Hunter's for years, and they shared many adventures . . . only some of which can be recounted here.

Ed was a large figure in the Aspen scene in the seventies and eighties. He knew the right people and traveled in the best circles. By "the best," I mean the most fun. Celebrities would come to town to visit *him*.

The legend began while Ed was an undergraduate at Notre Dame. Dick Kienast, who would later become sheriff of Pitkin County, was also a student there at the time. Both attended lectures by the philosopher Mortimer Adler. When they ended up

Doc and Ed having prettied themselves up with lipstick. Ed with Deborah and Cleverly, who are pretty enough without lipstick.

in Aspen they had a lot in common. Ed was introduced to many people through his classmate, and it snowballed from there. Kienast became sheriff, but he wasn't a regular cop. He was in the vanguard of progressive law enforcement in the Roaring Fork Valley, with his policies earning him the nickname "Dick Dove" and garnering him the attention of the national media. Tim Charles, a mutual friend, introduced Ed to Dr. Hunter S. Thompson. Ed and Hunter became close friends and remained so until Hunter's death. They shared many of the same hobbies, some of which Ed turned into a profession. Hence, the tour in Lompoc.

Ed became a solid citizen upon graduation from the federal penal system. He left the valley to pursue an honest living and he would occasionally use his famous friends as references.

Hunter was a fiercely loyal friend. Was he a good job reference? That remains an open question.

Here . . . you decide:

URGENT

Oct 9'91
Owl Farm

Carl Rhyan
Chairman, Nominating Committee
Illinois Trucking Associations

Dear Carl,

What the fuck are you trying
to prove by calling me up on the goddamn
telephone in the middle of the night &
asking Rude, Personal questions about
my old friend, Ed Hoban, who has paid
his debt to Society & doesn't need a
shit-eating Pig like you rooting around
in the ash-heap of his Private Life.

Don't fuck with me, Carl. I
hate Nazis & I usually kill what I hate.
You didn't invite me to the Annual Con-
vention this year, but I'll be there
anyway-- and if you do anything Queer
or Treacherous to endanger Ed's seat
on The Board, I'll catch you like a
weasel in one of those cheap grey stalls
in the Men's Room & slit yr. fucking
throat.

You won't know me, Carl -- but
I'll sure as hell know you.

OK, Take care. Sincerely,

R. Duke, Esq
General Counsel

cc: Ed Hoban
Tony Gill

MAN SUCKED

THROUGH

11-INCH

WATER PIPE

OK / send

Doc

Be careful when you ask Hunter for a favor.

In the late seventies and early eighties there were entrepreneurial types in the Roaring Fork Valley, people who had a little land and a little privacy and took up subsistence farming. Ed was one of them. He owned an old farmhouse in Emma, a half-hour drive from Woody Creek. At some point there actually had been a town of Emma, but that was long ago. By the time Ed purchased his house there, Emma was pretty close to the middle of nowhere. So he became involved with agribusiness, though what he was growing couldn't be purchased at the local farmers' market. Ed had inside plants flourishing in a greenhouse next to the garage and outside plants in a patch behind the barn. He was a good entrepreneur. A good farmer.

Late one summer, as harvest time was growing near, Ed's girlfriend decided that he wasn't providing her with enough walking-around money. She thought a garage sale was the answer. This was fine with Ed. Everyone has too much crap. The two went through eons of forgotten and unwanted junk, earmarking this and that for the sale. The Saturday morning of the event, Ed responsibly covered the greenhouse with a huge blue tarp. Not wanting to witness the detritus of his life being hawked in a driveway, he left to spend the day in Aspen.

Even before the first early-bird yard-sale aficionados arrived, the tarp had blown off the greenhouse. His girlfriend, focusing on sales, was oblivious, leaving the beautiful bushy plants exposed for one and all to see.

Ed's crops were low-maintenance, requiring little effort once they took hold; in fact, they grew like weeds. Babysitting was the problem. Farmer Ed liked to step out more than your average man of the soil does. He'd go up to Aspen, and some nights wouldn't come home at all. Sometimes he'd forget to make it home for days at a time. This would leave his crop home alone. To some, this might seem like careless parenting—giving your nymphomaniac teenage daughter her own van and a Gold Card. But to Ed it was a simple matter of trusting his fellow man. Those with a high opinion of human nature are often disappointed. And so it was that when Ed returned home one morning and went out to the greenhouse to tell the kids he was back, he found his babies gone. It was a crushing economic blow. Which is the same as a crushing emotional blow.

The outside patch behind the barn had been left unmolested for whatever reason. Probably a dead-of-night operation. The criminals had taken only what they had observed from the

Ed, the gentleman farmer.

Photographs by Nancy Cook Kelly, courtesy of Ed Hoban

Farmer Hoban enjoying the fruits of his labor.

driveway at the yard sale. There's not much one can do in these situations. But then, over the next couple of weeks, Ed noticed that the outside patch seemed to be shrinking, too. He actually counted the plants and, after a while, determined that the criminals were sneaking back and taking a couple of plants at a time. Ed and a friend erected a small tent in the middle of the patch. The pot was much taller than the tent, so it was invisible till you were right on top of it. Ed began sleeping in the patch. A friend would bring him young women for amusement. Sadly, a man like Ed can spend only so many nights in a tent, even with pleasant diversions to keep him company. One morning he returned from town to find half the crop gone.

Hunter was one of the first people whom Ed called. He needed some sympathy. Hunter was furious. What the fuck kind of world were we living in? Doc immediately declared war. There were two important issues at hand: To protect the remaining crop. First things first. And, beyond that, the ever-popular revenge. Retribution, reprisal, vengeance, comeuppance and getting even. Serious business.

One evening a few days later there was gunfire in Emma. Hunter was speeding up the road in the Shark, radio blaring, firing a pistol in the air. He pulled into Ed's driveway with presents for him: a .410 single shotgun, a two-thousand-candlepower boat/car light, two TV cameras, and a closed-circuit monitor. Everyone involved was confident that this equipment was sufficient to "do the trick." Optimism was running high.

Hunter heard nothing from Ed for a couple of weeks. It was harvest time, and Ed was pretty busy. There had been no more raids on the field, so Ed was just tending to his agribusiness. Hunter felt that he had a vested interest in the crop now and he was getting a little edgy about the lack of communication. Night after night he decided to give Ed a call and ended up putting it off each time. Finally he couldn't stand it anymore and drove out to Emma in the wee hours. He left this note stuck to Ed's front door with a dagger through it:

Ed 10/29/81

I can't believe that you lost those things that I left here . . . but in fact you owe

1. HST—one .410 single shotgun
2. HST—one 2k candlepower light—boat/car/etc.
3. John Kent—one closed-circuit TV set (2 cameras, one monitor)
4. HST—one blue chip elbow

An elbow is code for "lb." A pound of first-class pot.

Ed hadn't lost anything; it was just Hunter's way of conveying his sense of urgency. He must have been running out of dope. Actually a friend had borrowed the shotgun, for purposes neither Ed nor anyone else wanted to know. Ed could get it back anytime, if he didn't mind being in possession of evidence.

Ed was part of Hunter's posse. Back then Hunter traveled with a sort of entourage. They were all buddies, and Hunter treated them like equals, not minions.

During this time there was a rich Arab who lived up in the Starwood subdivision. The guy, in his mid-forties, liked to entertain, and he entertained people he considered to be important. Hunter fit the bill, so he would get invited to the guy's mini-castle for *Monday Night Football*. Along with Hunter would come Ed and the other members of Hunter's posse; also along with Hunter would come Hunter's gun. Hunter was going through a phase where he would always be "packing" when he

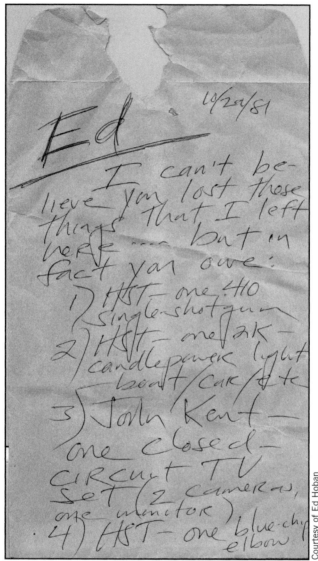

Courtesy of Ed Hoban

Cleverly kept trying to remind Hunter that "one man's souvenir is another man's evidence."

went out. No one else in the posse felt the need to carry a gun, and no one could put a finger on exactly why Hunter thought that he had to carry a gun. It was just a phase; it was Hunter. The gun could lead to the occasional awkward situation, as occurred with the Arab.

At the mini-castle, as a rule, bodyguards carried guns; the guests did not. The bodyguards felt they could function most effectively when they were the only ones armed. Sounds a little insecure, but there you are. These guys also performed household staff duties—butler, valet parking, coat checkers, waiters. The sorts of services we hope maybe to get when we go out and splurge is what rich Arabs demand 24/7. Mostly, though, they were bodyguards. Unlike a regular household staff, who would stay at the house when the boss went out, these fellas traveled wherever the boss went. They were always packing and had the look of men with virtually no sense of humor. Undoubtedly a plus in that line of work.

At the house, the guards would never do anything as gauche as patting guests down, so they didn't become aware of Hunter's pistol until after the first couple of Monday-night events. The topic came up when Hunter, ever the populist, decided to engage one of them in conversation. He must have felt that a common talking point would be weaponry, so he asked the guy what his firearm of choice was. That was no problem. The problem arose when Hunter drew his gun to compare. The bodyguards clearly found this disconcerting, judging from their response. I guess no guest had ever whipped out a piece in the presence of the Arab before. From that night on, while Ed and everyone else were checking their coats, Hunter was asked to check his gun.

After graduating from Lompoc, Ed took up the straight life in Chicago. He proved to be as good at making an honest living as he was at the other kind. He and Hunter were in regular contact via phone, fax, and e-mail. Hunter had set up meetings with his Chicago friends for Ed, to help smooth his transition back into the world. Hunter's Chicago friends became Ed's friends, so they were all excited when they learned that Doc's next speaking tour would bring him to Chicago.

The guys made the appropriate plans and fêted Hunter to a fare-thee-well when he got to town. The day after the lecture, and the partying that followed, Hunter was enjoying some down time at Ed's apartment. He noticed and was appreciating Ed's new black leather jacket. It was a cross between what you'd see a "button man" wearing in a gangster movie and your standard storm trooper issue. What Hunter admired most were the large flap pockets. They had to be ten inches square, roomy. Roominess was a quality that Hunter greatly admired in pockets, as he traveled with equipment that wasn't always 100 percent legal and was sometimes bulky. Obviously, bulging pockets were a drawback: probable cause. He asked Ed where he might acquire such a jacket. North Beach Leather, a shop whose owner happened to be a friend of Ed's. North Beach Leather was located in the Watertower mall on Michigan Avenue. The Watertower is a vertical mall. Up and down, not spread out like suburban malls. One travels it by elevator or escalator, not by hiking around the acreage.

When Ed and Hunter arrived at the mall, all the elevators were packed—a bad start. The full elevators necessitated them taking the escalator. Hunter never liked rubbing up against a lot of people, especially people who had no idea who he was. North Beach was on the seventh floor, which meant an awful lot of human contact for Doc. Up one escalator, off it, on to the next. Hunter's mood was changing.

When they arrived at the shop, Ed introduced Hunter to his friend, the owner, who, in turn, introduced Hunter to whatever employees were in the immediate area. The whole thing was becoming an event, with other salespeople and curious shoppers gathering around. It was having a bad effect on Hunter. The little group made its way to the rack of SS "button man" jackets. Ed's friend sized Hunter up, selected one, and helped Hunter into it. Hunter's perceptions were often colored by his mood, and his mood had gone south, far south. It had all become too big a project. "This is the ugliest thing I've ever seen. I wouldn't pay ten dollars for this piece of shit."

The crowd dispersed, and Hunter and Ed went back to Ed's for some more down time.

People close to Ed and Hunter are sure that this wisdom passed on to President Clinton proved to be invaluable.

THE WHITE HOUSE
WASHINGTON

May 28, 1993

Hunter S. Thompson
Owl Farm
Woody Creek, Colorado 81656

Dear Doc:

Thanks for the drawing you faxed me. I
appreciate the inspiration, and I intend to
keep working until the last dog dies.

Sincerely,

Bill

*Ed—
Yr. fey little
cartoon (pg. 2) now
hangs in the Oval
Office, for good
or ill.*

The leader of the free world and a clearly simpatico human being.

Cleverly Tells a Few Animal Stories

Peafowl, Dogs, and Cats

There was something odd about the Dobermans' gait as they loped across the lawn toward my truck. As the two dogs came closer, I realized what had happened and I knew that these would be the last dogs to reside at Owl Farm. When they were gone, there would be no replacements.

Hunter was mistrustful of the "establishment." His rules were his own and often didn't quite dovetail with those of the people who ran things. And next to law enforcement, banks and bankers are pretty much right at the heart of the mainstream establishment. Doc didn't care for bankers. He didn't like handing over his money to that kind of person. How could you trust them?

As with many people in the arts, Hunter's income was sporadic: feast or famine. As his fame grew, this situation became less pronounced, but even as recently as the seventies it was still the general fiscal pattern. Upon receiving the occasional large cash injection, he would, of course, give some thought to paying the bills. Then he'd stock up on the things that he'd been denying himself. And then his thoughts would turn to savings. Looking to the future, retirement. Krugerrands were Hunter's version of a 401k. He would bury them in ammo canisters in the yard. Stealing out in the wee hours, on moonless nights, shovel and canisters in hand, he'd dig, carefully removing the sod, and replacing it when the burial was complete. The dogs were the only witnesses. (You can see where this is heading.) Dogs love to dig. Dogs have good memories when it comes to this sort of thing, and always have great noses. Over a period of time it became clear that the Dobies had been digging around looking for the ammo canisters. Hunter felt he had to deal with the problem. So, today, their awkward gait was caused by the boxing gloves that he had duct-taped onto their front paws. This was a serious impediment to their digging, and didn't make loping any walk in the park either.

As expected, when these two went to their reward, and passed into legend, they weren't replaced. But the potential for a security breach was unacceptable. It was the beginning of the era of the peacocks.

Peacocks are excellent watchdogs. They squawk and screech at the least little thing—without the digging. Perfect for Owl Farm. Collectively speaking, they're called peafowl; the females are peahens, and the males are peacocks. We always referred to them as "the peacocks," though. Gender be damned. No one at Owl Farm was particularly concerned about offending the 4H Club.

The inventory of birds at Owl Farm would always vary, depending on a number of factors. Attrition due to predator interest was one significant factor. The peacocks were a link in the food chain, waiting to be consumed. The predator population of Woody Creek is diverse. Of course there were countless coyotes; they were ubiquitous. Then there were the foxes; they were always the prime suspects when a peacock went missing. This because when a bird was done in, the culprit would usually return on subsequent nights looking for more of the same. Hunter would trap the peacock killer, and nine tenths of the time it was a fox. Hunter would use something called a "live trap." This was exactly what the name implies. A live trap neither kills nor injures an animal. The trapper has the option of carting the critter away and setting it loose, or, if he's less a gambler and wants to rid himself of the creature forever, he has a target that's hard to miss. There were days when I arrived at Owl Farm to find a fox in one of the live traps, docile, awaiting its fate. Hunter's assistant, Deborah Fuller, who lived in the other cabin on the property, once told me that the foxes responded the same way to her, docile, resigned—but when Hunter would arrive to inspect the catch, they'd go nuts, snarling and frothing and pacing. How did they know? Hunter would give them a little lecture before he shot them; he thought he owed them that much, an explanation. It didn't seem to help. When I'd occasionally come upon one post mortem, its body would be frozen in such an attitude of crazed fury, with such an expression of viciousness and rage on its face, that there was no question about the creature having "gone gently into that good night."

Another factor that contributed to the peacock inventory at Owl Farm was, quite naturally, the birth rate. This would depend upon the number of mature females in residence any given spring, and on how many eggs each of the girls felt like laying. Of course there was more to the egg issue than just the laying. There were two perfectly good peacock pens, one attached to each of the cabins on the property. Sometimes the birds would see the logic in laying their eggs in the relative safety of the pens, sometimes not. When one of the ladies would choose to lay someplace totally unacceptable, like the backseat of the car someone was about to drive off in, the eggs had to be moved. This happened more often than you'd expect. When it did happen, it fell to Hunter to transport the eggs.

Peacocks are pretty friendly birds. They recognize you and actually seem capable of forming a bond with people they're used to. Hunter was truly fond of them, and it seemed that the affection was reciprocated to some degree. The peahens' warm feelings for Hunter, however, did not suffice for them to tolerate egg snatching.

One warm spring afternoon I pulled into Owl Farm to find Hunter lurking. To find a man who's master of his domain lurking in his own yard gave me a moment's pause. Hunter explained that one of the birds had laid two eggs on the tractor. Since the tractor was used on a regular basis, this was a fairly stupid place to set up a nursery. Hunter was waiting for the bird to decamp so he could grab the eggs and move them to the safety of one of the cages. Once the eggs were moved, the mother would usually accept the new spot and proceed with her nesting duties there. Hunter and I waited and watched. The bird came strutting out of the garage where the tractor was parked. When it was a safe distance from the garage, and occupied with its pecking and scratching, Hunter made his way inside. He came out with an egg in each hand and casually made for the cage on the deck of his cabin, feigning exaggerated nonchalance. The peacock spotted him. Then she spotted the eggs. With an ear-splitting screech, she gave chase. Hunter jumped, then fled. The peacock stayed on the ground, flapping as she ran, closing the distance between them. At the last possible moment she took flight, landing directly on Hunter's head. They both screeched, equally terrified, equally surprised. A peacock's talons are about the size of your hand, with large, sharp claws, Hunter's hands were full of peacock eggs. He had no way to dislodge her. He was not happy.

I don't know how good peacocks are, in general, at take-offs and landings; when I see them, they're usually just walking around pecking and squawking. This one seemed mighty surprised to be sitting on Hunter's head. I got the sense that she wanted off just as much as Hunter wanted her off. She flapped again and was back on the ground. Hunter lurched up the stairs and across the deck to the cage. He deposited the eggs, and the bird came flapping after. Hunter shut the door on bird and eggs. He stepped back, shaken and sweating.

Years later I moved into Hunter's neighborhood. My cabin was less than a mile from Owl Farm. One morning I looked out into the backyard and saw one of Hunter's birds strutting around. As a rule, the peacocks stuck close to Hunter's, the food source. Once in a while, though, one would wander off a bit, never too far, and get disoriented. I don't think their homing instincts are really great. To make it all the way to my place seemed unusual, but that was what happened. I called Owl Farm, and Deborah told me that Hunter was out of town. I explained the bird situation. Since neither of us considered ourselves peacock wranglers, we decided that Deborah would provide me with peacock chow and I'd feed the bird at my place until Hunter got back. Then he could figure it out.

When Hunter returned I described to him what pleasant company the bird had been. When I got up, it would be waiting outside the back door for a breakfast feeding. When I returned in the afternoon, at first it would be nowhere to be seen, but then it would appear when it realized I was home, and start looking for a little dinner. If I spent the remainder of the afternoon on the deck, it would hang out with me until I retired. I think that Hunter was charmed by the fact that one of his friends actually understood his feelings for these birds. So he offered to give the bird to me. Now, behavior that is regarded as eccentric in the talented and famous can actually be "probable cause" in a commitment hearing for the rest of us. I had to decline. I also didn't think that the uneasy truce between the peacock and my murderous cats would last forever. I appreciated that the huge bird was teaching the evil bird-killing cats a little humility, but I was afraid of what might happen if someone got brave.

Hunter suggested that I start feeding the bird a little closer to the back door every day. He figured I could eventually get it to eat in my back room, and then I could trap it in there, at which time Hunter would come over, bag the thing, and transport it back to Owl Farm. It took a little over a week, but in the end the bird was eating comfortably in the back room, and I could close the door behind it without upsetting it.

It took another week to get Hunter over to my house. I'd call Doc at seven or eight in the morning, when the bird was feeding. If Hunter picked up the telephone at seven in the morning, it's important to remember that it was the *end* of his day, not the beginning. Heck, no one's at his best at the end of a hard day. Same with Hunter. So it took a few tries for me to catch him in the mood to chase a peacock around my back room. Then one morning he said, "Anita and I will be right over."

They arrived a little later. Hunter was fully equipped. He had a very large tumbler of scotch, a hash pipe, a cocaine grinder, and, oh yes, an old blanket with which to bag the bird. Hunter prepared himself to do battle. A little of this; some of that; a bit of this, that, and something else; and, yes, the blanket. We peeked into the back room to observe the bird. It was completely calm and at home. Anita and I backed off. Hunter slipped into the room and closed the door behind him. Soon the screaming started: the peacock's high-pitched shrieks and Hunter's lower pitched sputtering. Both in a rapid staccato. No actual words discernible from either one. Anita and I sat on my couch looking at each other, waiting. The melee went on and on. No one expected this to be pretty, but we were becoming concerned. Suddenly, silence.

Hunter emerged with the bird wrapped in the blanket. A peacock will become totally docile when enveloped in this kind of darkness. I walked Hunter and Anita and the bird to their car. Back in the cabin I inspected my back room. There was peacock shit everywhere. Not just the horizontal surfaces—the walls and even the ceiling were well smeared. While I was pondering how even such a large bird could emit so much dung, the phone rang. It was Hunter reporting that the peacock seemed fine, totally unscathed. He and Anita were going to turn in and he'd call in the evening. I promised to visit my friend, the peacock, very soon.

Liz Treadwell was one of the great beauties in a town full of beautiful women. She was beautiful in the old days, and she's still beautiful now. Lucky us. Back in the day, she was linked romantically with a number of people in the entertainment industry whose names you'd recognize. She is currently hitched to a very good man, a real cowboy.

Liz loved animals, all of them, so when she suggested to Hunter that she cook peacock for the gang for Thanksgiving dinner, Hunter was the only one who even pretended to take her seriously. She said it to bait him, to get his goat. Hunter's goat deserved to be got, as he was usually on the giving end of the goat-getting.

Liz was six months pregnant. She was always known as a terrific cook, so "the boys" decided that dinner with her was a truly inspired idea. Liz started cooking at first light. Being knocked up, she'd been leading the pure life and didn't have anything better to do. By late afternoon the guys started to straggle in. It was opening day of ski season, and that's what most of them had been doing. What Hunter had been doing until then is up for speculation. With the first arrival, the booze was broken out, along with everything else it takes to have a happy holiday, and no one seemed interested in holding back. Liz was preparing a full-blown, all-the-fixings dinner, and had been at it for about ten hours; her guests seemed bent on getting fucked up as quickly as possible.

By the time the feast was ready, the group was far, far gone. The huge dining room table was covered by a meal out of Norman Rockwell, and no one was hungry. Liz was a little bit cranky. No, it was worse than that: her back hurt, she'd been on her feet for hours. She was homicidal. Liz's classic beauty concealed an iron will and a nicely evolved temper; she was not one to fuck with. She watched the lads "not eating" for as long as she could stand it, cartoon steam coming out of her ears. She finally turned aside to feed her two Australian shepherds, Josh and Jilly, essentially to put off the wringing of necks that was next on her agenda. When she returned from the kitchen, the boys were still lounging around the living room, sprawled on sofas and easy chairs, having a good old giggle, and still ignoring the food. There were no other women at the gathering. Liz decided to take the passive approach, expelled some steam, and started clearing the untouched food from the table. Halfway through the clearing process, the guys decided they were hungry. Liz was about to blow. Hunter was sitting on the sofa smoking, which added to the exhausted, sober, pregnant Liz's rage. Suddenly, the pooches came flying in from the kitchen; Liz turned around and saw Hunter with a can of lighter fluid in his hand.

Courtesy of Elizabeth Treadwell

Photograph of Hunter taken by Liz Treadwell at an occasion involving less tension than the ill-fated Thanksgiving dinner.

Hunter used to do this trick in which he would put some lighter fluid in his mouth and squirt it out between his teeth while igniting it. It created an impressive stream of flame. This was the trick he was performing just as one of the dogs came charging up to him seeking a little affection. The result was a line of fire straight down the dog's back from the base of its neck to its tail. The dog screamed, Liz screamed, Hunter screamed, everyone else either jumped straight into the air or froze in place. The flaming dog bolted for the door that Liz opened just in time for the animal to charge through and roll crazily in the snow.

Fortunately the dog was uninjured. The lighter fluid burned so fast it never got down to the hide. After the initial shock, the

boys regained their composure and, in the spirit of true profes-
sionalism, acted as if nothing at all had happened and went back
to whatever joke they were telling or conversation they were having before the conflagration. No one commented on the event at
all. Hunter never apologized. The nauseating stench of burned
dog hair that permeated the room was never acknowledged as
the happy group finally sat down to the traditional Thanksgiving
dinner Liz had spent so much time preparing.

Liz tells the story about her good friend Fiona who returned to
Aspen after an extended stay in Australia and rented a house
across the road from Hunter. Soon after taking up residence,
Fiona called Liz and told her that there were mice everywhere.
Liz told her to get a cat. Fiona knew that Liz had an inventory of
cats and asked if she could borrow one. Liz explained that you
don't loan out your cats and that Fiona should go to the animal
shelter and adopt one. For some reason Fiona was determined to
borrow a cat instead of adopting, and actually managed to find
someone to loan her one. It was huge, fifteen pounds of black and
tan stripes, white chest, and a black mask just like a raccoon's,
a real mouse terminator. The cat did fine work, and before long
Fiona's mouse issues were a thing of the past.

While there were plenty of mice to hunt, the cat was happy to
stay close to home, but when it finally ran out of prey it started
to explore the neighborhood. One night it found its way on to
Hunter's deck. The peacocks pitched a fit; they had no idea what
to make of a cat the size of a Volkswagen.

The next morning Fiona opened her door, and in staggered
the cat, beaten and bloody. She rushed the poor beast to the
vet to find that it was riddled with birdshot. The cat survived
but sustained some permanent brain damage, and the vet's bill

was well into four figures. HUNTER, WHY THE FUCK DID YOU SHOOT MY CAT? was the phrase heard echoing through Woody Creek . . . more than once. The thing was, it wasn't Fiona's cat; it was a loaner. She had been given this huge, beautiful mouse-killing machine and now had thousands of dollars in vet bills and a cat who wasn't quite the same as when she'd borrowed it. As usual Hunter admitted nothing. He had absolutely no idea what she was talking about. Cats that looked like raccoons? Sounded pretty far-fetched to him.

Fiona paid the vet nonetheless, the cat's owners were displeased, and the poor addled cat led a very pampered life to the end of its days.

Braudis Describes Hunter's "Hey, Rube" Moment

It was mid-afternoon, about three thirty; I was in my office. The phone rang, and it was Hunter. He and his assistant, Deborah, were at the bar at the Jerome.

Through the eighties and nineties, Deborah Fuller was Hunter's director of operations, hostess, executive secretary, bouncer, and mother. She lived in the cabin next to his house. As part-time assistants and lovers came and went, Deborah remained the constant, a woman beyond price and without whom nothing could happen at Owl Farm. On his own, Hunter was helpless. Deborah knew all and did all; she was loyal, fierce, and loving. She was the gatekeeper and the game warden. She knew Hunter better than anyone, and made it all work.

That afternoon Hunter asked me if I would care to join them. Of course I would. The Jerome had been Hunter's campaign headquarters in 1970 and the hundred-year-old bar with high ceilings, a cracked tile floor, and great views through huge windows was a favorite of us all. The bar is a block away from the courthouse where I had my office, so I said I would meet them in five minutes. I walked in, pulled up a stool between them, and bummed a Dunhill from Hunter. The J-Bar was the last establishment in Aspen that still allowed smoking, a prerequisite for Hunter's business. It also boasted a Tom Benton THOMPSON FOR SHERIFF poster on the wall.

Tom Benton had been one of Hunter's best friends for forty years. His art was political and strong. Mostly silk-screen prints, in limited editions, his posters supported candidates or causes, or were against war. Hand-carved letters spelling out quotes like "Eat the rich" or "First we kill all the lawyers" mixed with beautiful graphics and color.

The THOMPSON FOR SHERIFF posters featured a double-thumbed fist clenching a peyote button, and decades after the election they were still in demand. Hunter had a deal with Benton. Hunter believed that he owned the art. He had been right there when the poster was conceived and probably had as much to do with the look of the thing as anyone. Hunter had his own very specific notions about graphics and design and wasn't shy about scribbling away on anyone's work, whether it was Tom Benton's or Ralph Steadman's. He would give Benton 50 percent of any revenues generated by the sale of the posters that Benton screened in his studio. The posters were available in some galleries and on the Internet. If the art was signed by Hunter, the price per poster went from one hundred dollars to three hundred dollars.

Courtesy of Deborah Fuller

Hunter with Tom Benton and an HST FOR SHERIFF signed for outgoing police chief Tom Stephenson.

Photograph by Deb Fuller, courtesy of Ed Hoban

Kitchen camaraderie with Doc, Ed Hoban, and artist Paul Pascarella, codesigner of the fist logo.

Tom Benton's wife, Marcy, handled the money end of their poster business. She would deliver product and get the dough, more or less treating the whole thing like a drug deal. Benton stayed in the studio or worked for me as an officer in the Pitkin County jail.

One night, years before, while Benton was on duty in the jail, Hunter called him to ask if the jail had cable. Yes, the jail had cable TV; Owl Farm didn't. There was a title fight available only on cable and at nine thirty that night the inmates were locked down. Hunter came to the jail with his Dunhills and Chivas, and he and Benton watched the fight. It was a good measure of their friendship.

Anyway, Hunter, Deborah, and I were sitting at the bar when Joey DiSalvo, my chief detective and a friend of Hunter's, walked in. He was carrying a signed poster, recently purchased from Marcy Benton. It was signed not by HST, but by Marcy Benton. In gold Magic Marker. It was an obviously butchered attempt to replicate Doc's signature. When Joey unrolled the forgery, Deborah sighed. "That bitch." I grinned, and Hunter started fuming.

Throughout his career Hunter felt that he had been ripped off by agents, publishers, and business managers. His paranoia and perception made him a wolverine if he had anything in his hands resembling evidence. He now had some serious evidence.

I said that Tom probably didn't know that Marcy might be signing art with Hunter's "HST." Hunter's only focus was on the two hundred dollars he was losing and the fraud that had been perpetrated upon the buyer. We ordered another round of drinks, and Hunter promised Joey an authentic version. I happened to glance at the rear entrance to the bar, and there was Marcy walking with a man in a suit and tie. She was carrying a heavy roll of papers under her arm. It had to be business. She and the client sat at a table directly behind us, oblivious to our presence. She was making a deal.

I leaned forward, elbows on the bar, and whispered to Hunter and Deb, "Don't look now, but you won't believe who just sat down behind us." Of course Deb and Hunter immediately craned their necks and looked over their shoulders toward the table. Marci caught the glance and waved daintily. Who could believe this? Well, Hunter could. With creaky motions, he slid off the stool and stood. I said, "Hunter, don't do anything you'll regret." Hunter sauntered over to Marcy and the mark. His voice rose, and Marcy blushed. She quickly gathered her art and exited through the door that she had come in, with the "suit" in tow.

Hunter had been involved in more than a few brawls in this very bar, and a simple yelling match instead of a donnybrook suited me fine. Hunter ordered more drinks, asked the bartender for a pen, and started writing something on a napkin. I walked out the rear door and into the lobby. Out there, I spotted Marci, handing the man in the suit four "signed" posters and taking twelve hundred dollars in cash. I approached them and said to the man, "I'm sure Hunter told you that this isn't his signature."

"Yeah," he said, "that is clear. But I'm from Hong Kong, and the art is good and the people to whom I'm giving these as gifts don't know that Hunter didn't sign them." He said goodbye and went to his room. I gave Marci the "stink eye." She smiled and left the hotel.

When I returned to the bar, Hunter was still scribbling on the napkin, biting his tongue as he often did while creating. He eventually slid over to me what he had written: "Hey, Rube! This is a public warning that there is an active trade in forged art in Aspen, Colorado. Beware of making any purchase of any Hunter S. Thompson for Sheriff posters from a freak-like skank with black hair and a high blood-alcohol content." That was just for starters. It went on and got meaner. I asked him what he was going to do with it, and he said that he was going to place an ad in the *Aspen Times*. Fortunately for all of us, his warning never appeared in print.

Hunter toiling away on a "Hey, Rube" column.

Hunter's digital weekly column, published by ESPN.com, was entitled "Hey Rube." I always considered it an homage to that day's rage.

Tom Benton recently retired, for the third time, from his detention deputy position. His marriage to Marcy continued, and he also continued to make beautiful art. He crafted my campaign poster for the 2006 election. (I, unlike Hunter, was victorious, by the way.)

A Brief History of the Sheriff's Squeeze

Deanna Gay rolled into Aspen in the sixties. A hot, sixteen-year-old ski racer, she took one look around and instantly knew that she was home. Everyone called her DeDe. Back then in Aspen a lot of the streets were still dirt and there were few stoplights; there were no rules, all victimless "crimes" seemed legal, love was in the air, and no one's dictionary contained the term *statutory rape*. In some ways, it was paradise.

Skiers have always marched to the beat of their own drummers, and the faster you skied, the less you worried about what anyone thought. DeDe skied very fast, and while others were trying to keep up with the haute ski couture of the moment, she could be seen screaming down Aspen Mountain in plaid wool

Bermuda shorts and argyle knee socks. She blew away the best skiers and caught the attention of every lecher in town.

DeDe was a freshman at CU and ski-racing was the point of her being there. Her coach was ski legend Bob Beattie. His skiers and a lot of other people called him Coach; some of us called him Beats; to the world he was Mr. Skiing. He's largely responsible for the sport being what it is in the United States today. Hunter called him neighbor. Beattie moved in across the street from Hunter, and a friendship began that was as close as it was unlikely.

Young DeDe would watch Hunter holding court at the end of the Jerome Bar. Surrounded by friends, acolytes, and awestruck tourists, he seemed oblivious to her. Was it possible that Hunter Thompson was the only straight male in Aspen who wasn't trying to figure out how to get her into a snow cave? Or was he just playing it particularly cool? Either way, DeDe was not amused. She began to scheme.

Vodka gimlets were the popular drink of co-eds at the time, and that is exactly what she proceeded to pour down her sexy, underage gullet . . . in quantity. Finally emboldened, she headed for Hunter's end of the bar, set to get an invitation to Owl Farm. Amazingly she wasn't having much success until a mutual friend, Chris Hanson, came into the picture. Chris was handsome, tanned, and had a great Cheshire cat smile. He was a ski instructor and a cowboy. He could hold his own with Hunter drinking or doing whatever else came up. He could also hold his own roping, riding, and shooting, and was great with a bullwhip. After a whole bunch more drinks, it was decided that Chris could take a cigar out of DeDe's mouth with a whip. This experiment could only be done at Owl Farm, a small victory for DeDe. Off they went with brains full of booze and hearts full of pure science.

DeDe stood gamely in front of the stone fireplace in Hunter's living room with a sacrificial Cohiba clenched between her teeth. She signaled the cowboy to proceed, hoping to impress Hunter with her fearlessness. No one present was more surprised than DeDe when there was a loud crack and the cigar simply disappeared. She was also fairly surprised that her face was still exactly where it belonged. Hunter must have been a little impressed as he took things to the next level. He bellowed, "Do you shoot, whatever your name is? And if you do, would you like to step outside and fire off a few rounds?" Thrilled beyond reason, DeDe answered that of course she shot. "Grandpa had a duck club. I've owned a gun all my life."

Bob and the "fair and winsome" DeDe (Deanna Gay) Brinkman.

Hunter was happy; this new one had spunk. "Let's put a few things on top of this propane tank," he said. "You can have the first shot. Don't mind propane, do you, young lady?" "Of course not. My dad was a gas man; I adore propane," DeDe gushed. Basically Hunter was hoping that the new girl would have enough sense to be scared to death by the prospect of shooting bottles off a five-hundred-gallon propane tank. In truth, DeDe's daddy actually was in the gas business and she knew that it would take a lot more muzzle velocity than what they were shooting with to penetrate the tank. Hunter did mention that it would be great if she didn't "point that fucking thing at me!" All the years in the duck blind hadn't prepared her for shooting under these conditions. She was winging it.

Things went well that afternoon, everyone had a good time, but the young ski goddess didn't become the fixture in the kitchen that she had hoped to be. This was probably for the best, as sometimes the kitchen had a bad effect on young people who hadn't developed their calluses. Years went by, and DeDe and Hunter enjoyed a nice friendship that didn't much involve him trying to get her into a snow cave.

In the eighties, the Aspen Art Museum started to have fundraisers in the form of art cart derbies. These were soapbox derbies for artists and pretty much anyone else with enough time on their hands to build gravity-powered racers. The course ran down Aspen Street from the bottom of Aspen Mountain's chairlift 1A to Main Street. That means it was steep and fast. The contests were judged on more than speed, though. Artistic merit, sexiness, and a number of other categories were just as important as velocity. There were spectacular crashes and questionable behavior of every sort. Naturally the event was wildly popular, drawing huge crowds and even national TV coverage.

Part of the event's popularity was the celebrity involvement; this was where DeDe came in. By the mid-eighties, she was close to the art crowd and the museum, and also deeply involved with Aspen's Hollywood expatriates. DeDe convinced her old coach Bob Beattie to announce the race. She recruited celebrity judges such as Michael Douglas, George Hamilton, and Emmy-winning screenwriter Tracy Keenan Wynn. The artist Tom Benton and then-sheriff Dick Kienast were also judges. A great lineup, but people wanted Hunter; this thing was custom made for Hunter. DeDe, it seemed, was the only girl for the job. Get Hunter.

At first Hunter was cagey. "I won't have to go on TV with George Hamilton, will I?" Hunter would soon learn that Hamilton was a very decent and hip guy. Hunter was basing his opinion of George on an image as carefully crafted as his own. DeDe tried to explain this to him, but Hunter always had to figure things out for himself, so she finally just conceded that Hunter wouldn't

Carter and the Stoli bottle, morphed into a Bud bottle. Art carters were shameless sluts and would alter their carts to accommodate anyone with an open checkbook.

Race action.

Photographs courtesy of Dick Carter

have to go on TV with anyone he didn't want to. Ever the negotiator, Hunter then demanded a more or less unlimited supply of liquor and drugs. This surprised no one, and had already been factored in as part of the cost of doing business. Whose budget it came out of, no one tells. It would have been difficult for Doc to blow the thing off; too many of his buddies were involved: Beattie announcing, Benton and Kienast judging, and artists Dick Carter and Michael Cleverly both racing in the competition.

Cleverly's Death Bat.

George Hamilton, awed by the Death Bat.

Michael Douglas, Tracy Keenan Wynn, and Doc, judging the entrants.

Carter had somehow conned a liquor distributor into sponsoring his racer. He built a huge fiberglass bottle of Stolichnaya vodka. It was very fast, and its great weight made it a potential hazard to both driver and spectators. All of the contestants needed to have steering and brakes—but the two weren't exactly at the top of anyone's list.

Cleverly was the team captain and driver for the Fedaykin Death Commandos, a group of prominent Aspenites who were successful, solid citizens on the surface but still depraved ex-hippie frat boys somewhere beneath and who had had the wherewithal to finance the Fedaykin Death Bat. They had stolen their name from the sci-fi classic *Dune*. Built by Cleverly and *Aspen Times* ace reporter Andy Stone, the Death Bat was a cross between a dragonfly, a square-rigger, a bat, and a biplane. It had multiple wings, propellers, and complicated masts and rigging. It looked dangerous and threatening. The logo for the Fedaykins was a high-tech skull with wings. The image most people associated with them was the baby blue nitrous oxide tank with several hoses extending from it that they kept in the pit area.

By the end of race weekend, DeDe had gained a lot of credibility with Hunter. He had a terrific time, spending as much of it as possible in the Fedaykin pit area with the nitrous tank. The fact that he was a judge prompted a few complaints of potential bias that were largely ignored. In point of fact, the Fedaykins had thoughtfully provided the announcers and all the judges with Fedaykin team uniforms. The announcers' T-shirts sported the Fedaykin logo with BIASED ANNOUNCER written underneath, and the judges' T-shirts had the words CORRUPT JUDGE under the logo. Kienast's T-shirt bore a skull with CORRUPT SHERIFF. The idea of favoritism was pretty much a moot point. On the back, the shirts all carried the slogan SAFETY THIRD. Hunter was happy: there was blood on the pavement and there were drugs in the Doctor. DeDe was tops.

By the late eighties, DeDe had parlayed her Hollywood connections into a business called Aspen Production Services. APS essentially hooked the Hollywood guys up with whatever they needed to be hooked up with in Aspen, and acted as liaison between production companies and the Aspen community, although she also provided the same service in other parts of the world.

In 1991 Brandon Tartikoff and NBC decided to produce an Aspen movie. It was to be written by John Byrum. Byrum was a huge Hunter fan and had met the Doctor on a visit to Aspen. The film was supposed to be based on a Hunter-type character using Hunter language and involving whacky Hunter-type scenarios and "gonzo" events. DeDe and her crew were told not to mention any of this to Hunter under any circumstances.

The phone call DeDe inevitably got from Owl Farm was packed with expletives and threats. "How could you align yourself with these sadistic Hollywood pig fucks capitalizing on my life?" DeDe first denied everything, "Why would you think that?" Later: "How did you find out?"

Trying to outwit Hunter was futile. Occasionally flattery could be employed, but not here. When Hunter felt exploited, no amount of cajoling could placate him. The media was alerted; ugly phone calls were traded back and forth; there were newspaper articles.

It was too late for the production company to back off; they were already in too deep. Crews were in town, locations had been arranged, the actors were cast. All DeDe could do was make the best of a bad situation. She did her job and cast her future boyfriend, then-deputy Bob Braudis, as Deputy Cujo. The movie was a piece of shit; no one saw it.

For some reason Hunter forgave DeDe. In fact, the event was never mentioned between them. Perhaps even back then Hunter could see that somewhere down the road, his best friend, Bob, and the crazy hottie DeDe would get together. On into their dotage.

Hunter's Adventures with "Duke," a Gentleman of Dubious Character

Duke's phone rang at 3:00 A.M. "DukethisisHunter, whatareyou-doing?" Hunter may have been the only person on planet earth who could ask that question, at that hour, and not be accused of being disingenuous. In Hunter's world there were lots of things one might reasonably be doing at 3:00 A.M. As it happened, Duke was awake. "Just hanging out, hoping a couple girls might stop by."

Did Duke have an actual reason to expect that a couple of girls might stop by? Or was it because any single guy who's awake at 3:00 A.M. is going to be hoping that a couple of girls might stop by? What else are you going to be hoping for?

Hunter went on, "HowaboutifIcomeover? Doyouhaveany-thingtodrink?"

"Where the hell are you?" asked Duke, justifiably. Duke lived miles from Owl Farm, but only about eight blocks from the Jerome Bar, where Hunter turned out to be. He must have been doing his good deed for the day, helping the bartender close up or something of that nature. We won't ask.

Duke said that he might have a couple beers. Hunter said, "GreatI'llbeoverinafew."

Courtesy of Missy Erlanger

Duke Dixon and Doc enjoying
Monday Night Football levity.

Half an hour later there was a knock on the door of Duke's East Hopkins Avenue apartment. He opened the door, there was a huge potted plant standing there waiting to be let in. He jumped back. Absent LSD, visits from potted plants at that hour were rare, and a touch frightening. Duke studied the plant for a moment. It resembled ones that he'd encountered in the lobby of the Hotel Jerome. Just as he began to feel a little less uneasy, the plant spoke: "Jesuschrist-

lemmethefuckin. Takethisthingforgodssake." The plant wanted to come in. Duke opened the door wide, and the plant walked in, with Hunter Thompson directly behind it.

"WherethehellcanIputthis?" It was just Hunter carrying an enormous plant. That wasn't so bad. "Anywhere you want, Hunter." Hunter put the mammoth display of foliage on the coffee table. Duke was worried; could the table handle the weight? "Whathaveyougottodrink?" Duke went to the refrigerator. "Beer." "Nevermind, Ibroughtthis." Hunter opened his coat and hauled out a large, industrial-size jug of vanilla extract. This was exactly why a lot of us had always thought that Hunter's innards should qualify as a Superfund site. Duke asked himself why someone would swipe a jug of vanilla extract from the Jerome kitchen when one could just as easily swipe booze from the bar? He didn't bother to pose this question to Hunter. Vanilla extract *is* 12 percent alcohol, but still . . .

By 9:00 A.M. things were winding down. Duke had finished his beer and Hunter had put an impressive dent in the vanilla extract. The girls, real or imagined, had not yet materialized. Hunter was hosting a luncheon later that day at Owl Farm, and Duke was to be in attendance. The boys decided that the gals probably weren't going to show, and called it a night.

Hunter's fête the next afternoon was in honor of Semmes Luckett's eighty-year-old mother. Mrs. Luckett was a true daughter of the South and had raised a Southern gentleman. She had long wanted to meet the famous writer from Louisville, Hunter S. Thompson.

Semmes was a close friend of Jack Nicholson, who was, of course, close to Hunter. Semmes was overseeing a construction project at Nicholson's Aspen home and was a fixture at the J-Bar and other Aspen haunts. Hunter and Semmes were friends, so when his mom came for a visit, it was natural for Hunter to be gracious.

When Duke arrived at Owl Farm on his Harley with the

Drawing by Jack Nicholson

Hunter with six-pack, sketched by Jack Nicholson.

usual hot blonde on the back, the other guests were already in place on the deck. They didn't seem to mind the thin coat of driveway dust they were suddenly wearing courtesy of Duke and his motorcycle. As Duke and the babe climbed the steps to the deck, Hunter was busy wielding a machete, dissecting watermelons and cantaloupes that had been injected with liquor the night before. Dissecting is probably too elegant a term to use to describe what Hunter was doing. The chopping strokes he was using to cut up the melons would have decapitated an ox. A less trusting audience might have found it disconcerting, but those present were Southern aristocracy, and decorum wouldn't have allowed for unpleasant accidents.

The alcohol-infused fruit and good food made for a convivial meal. After lunch Mrs. Luckett turned to Hunter and, in her best Southern manner, asked him if she might have some small memento to remember the afternoon by. Doc was charmed by the request and cast about looking for something appropriate to give this eighty-year-old Southern belle. His glance fell on the wall behind them. There was a large, early-model stun gun/cattle prod. It looked more like a prop from a *Star Wars* movie than the nice compact devices the cops Taser us with nowadays. Doc kept it around to ensure civilized behavior. He ripped it off the wall and handed it to Mrs. Luckett, beaming all the way. Mrs. Luckett smiled and accepted the gift with only her bulging eyes betraying her feelings. Others at the table were clapping Hunter on the back and congratulating him on making such a fine choice. After a few moments Hunter asked Semmes Luckett's mother if she'd like him to show her how to operate the device. There was a long, pregnant silence. Mrs. Luckett pondered. Upon what occasion would she use it, and on whom? Her lack of response was beginning to make people uncomfortable. Could it be possible that the stun gun had been an inappropriate choice? It seemed so right. Hunter began to have second thoughts. He excused himself and disappeared into the house. He returned to the deck a few minutes later toting a lovely turquoise pendant.

Taking the cattle prod and handing Mrs. Lucket the pendant, he said, "Itoccurredtomethatyoumighthavetroublegettingitontheplane." It was clear that the only possible place Hunter could have come up with something like the pendant was his girlfriend's jewelry box. People chose to overlook that obvious conclusion and said nothing. Mrs. Luckett beamed with both relief and delight. Her thank-you note to Hunter mentioned that she had no trouble whatever getting the pendant on the plane home.

Weeks later Duke and some of Hunters close friends were in the kitchen watching *Monday Night Football,* where there was the usual drinking and gambling. At halftime Duke recounted the story of Semmes's mother, the lunch, and the gift. The consensus of opinion was that a Baretta would have been a better choice. A lighter weapon, better for an elderly woman. Smaller, more easily concealed in a clutch or a shawl, easier to smuggle on an airplane. Hunter waxed poetic about Mrs. Luckett's genteel grace, indicating that she reminded him of his own mother, whose birthday was that very day. The assembled lads asked what Hunter had given his mother for the occasion.

"Houston and four" was his reply.

New Orleans. Hunter was in town as part of a book tour. Coincidentally, Duke had also scheduled a trip to the Crescent City, for the jazz festival. They decided to hook up. Hunter had reserved several suites on the upper floors of the Pontchartrain Hotel. In the spirit of keeping order in the food chain, the attorney general of Louisiana was occupying a suite two floors below Hunter. Doc was the first of his party to arrive, so he was uncharacteristically alone, no supervision. He proceeded to run a bath and stretched out for a bit to begin the unwinding process.

It seemed as if the phone had been ringing for quite a while, but it was the pounding on the door that really brought him back to consciousness. He swung his feet off the bed, and when they hit the floor the water immediately soaked his socks. "What the . . . ?" The carpet was soaked. Hunter slogged to the door; the faces on the other side were concerned, agitated. "Are you all right?" they asked. "Of course I am, except the damn carpet is soaking, can you help?" At that point he became aware of the sound of running water coming from the bathroom. He asked, "Is there a leak? Has there been a mishap?" The hotel authorities excused themselves, passed him, and headed into the bathroom. Hunter followed. The tile floor was deep underwater. They turned the water off. "You'll have to move into a suite upstairs; the one below you is also soaked. The one below that, too, the one the attorney general was occupying." Hunter was annoyed by the thoughtlessness of this inconvenience, but decided not to complain. Give the fools a break.

When the rest of Hunter's entourage arrived, they found that they weren't staying in as close proximity as they had hoped, but Hunter assured them that there was a reasonable explanation and said no more. Duke called that evening. He asked to speak to Mr. Ackerman, and the hotel operator put him through to Hunter's room.

Duke was staying at a friend's apartment on Bourbon Street. They agreed that he would attend the following day's book signing and then the two would do something fun afterward.

When the signing wound down to stragglers and Hunter's party, Doc announced that he'd just as soon go off with Duke, so everyone else could do what they wanted with their evening. Hunter and Duke found themselves an excellent restaurant in the French Quarter. As was his usual practice, Hunter ordered a glass of ice water, a beer, a Bloody Mary, and a large Chivas on the rocks. In the spirit of excess, Duke ordered a beer. They enjoyed a good wine with dinner, confining themselves to one entrée each. As the busboy was clearing, Hunter asked about dessert specials.

"Crème brûlée," the waiter said.

"Hmm," Hunter said. "I'll have some." The waiter turned to leave. Hunter said, "Wait, keep going."

The waiter turned back to the table. "We also have mud pie."

"I'll try that," Hunter said and indicated that the waiter should proceed.

"Cheesecake."

"Sure, that sounds good."

"Pecan tort."

"Great."

"Our house special tonight is chocolate mousse."

"Nope, sounds a little too rich."

After dinner the two headed out into the Quarter. They had heard that there was an interesting joint on Royale. The boys made their way to "The Wild Side," a subterranean club with dark stairs leading down to the door.

Smoke and gloom greeted them as they entered. Even coming in from the night, their eyes had to adjust to the darkness. They identified the bar and groped off in that direction. Settling into the drinks, Hunter began to talk. As Duke's senses adjusted to the atmosphere, he began to get an odd vibe. Sure, the bartender is flagrantly gay. So? This was the city of anything goes. There was something else, though. Sounds emanating from the darkness. While Doc was happily chatting away, Duke was beginning to see into the shadows. He picked out faces, lots and lots of makeup. The darker the shadow, the stranger, more feral the sounds. Hunter was laughing, amused by his own banter. Duke was peering. The world of the club was slowly revealing itself to him. He grabbed Hunter's wrist. "Hunter, look around." Hunter stopped talking and swiveled his head, trying to zone in on whatever Duke wanted him to see. "See?" Duke lowered his voice to a whisper. "Hunter, everyone in here is gay or a transvestite or a transsexual, or all of it. There are people actually having sex in the corners." Hunter continued to look around. He nodded. "I'm happy."

The next night Hunter showed up at the Bourbon Street apartment where Duke was staying with three transvestites in tow. Word is, nothing happened.

Later, back in the kitchen at the farm, when Duke would try to recount the incident, he found Hunter a little uncooperative in helping with the details. Duke got the feeling that he shouldn't bring it up again, ever.

Hunter Takes an Artist to a Filthy Strip Joint

The artist Richard "Dick" Carter first met Hunter Thompson at a Christmas party around 1980. The party was at the home of fellow artist Missie Thorne. Predictably, the guests were painters, sculptors, and assorted artsy types. Hunter always felt a kinship with artists, and enjoyed their company. He wasn't quite as fond of "artsy" types.

At Missie's party, Hunter had sought refuge in a back room with a TV. He was watching a college basketball game when Carter wandered in. They started talking sports and hit it off, and began to make small proposition bets. This was always an excellent way to get to know Hunter—partly because of forging a bond in the common interest in sports, and partly because it was a way to start getting used to the fleecing, or attempted fleecing, as early on as possible.

Carter learned fast.

Carter and Hunter's next meeting was on the periphery of a heavyweight championship bout. It was the dark ages of techno television, and singer Jimmy Buffett was the man who had a satellite dish to receive the closed-circuit telecast. Everyone was going over to Buffet's to watch the fight. Hunter, a huge boxing enthusiast, was looking forward to the evening; Dick chose not to attend. It was one of those fights that was over far too quickly, and within minutes there was nothing left to do but party. As a rule, Hunter had no real problem with a good party, but a much-anticipated sporting event ending in disappointment left him a bit off his feed. He had to move on, so he called Carter.

Hunter had decided to interpret Dick's failure to attend the fight party as an act of great wisdom. He wanted to hook up with his new buddy who had had sense enough to stay home. In fact, Carter's real reasons for not going to the party were completely pedestrian: he didn't know Buffet that well, and he preferred to stay in his studio and work that evening. It didn't turn out that way.

Hunter always traveled with whatever he figured it would take to get him through the night. On this occasion it got them both through the night. How much progress—or, to be more correct, how little progress—the artist made on his painting was not the issue. It was an evening when schemes were schemed, plots were hatched. That's what counted.

A rich fool who lived nearby had installed a life-size white plastic statue of a rearing stallion in a pasture right next to the road. This beautiful manicured and fenced-in meadow would have been paradise to a horse with a pulse. No one knows how the synthetic steed felt about it. Some of the *Homo sapiens* in the neighborhood, however, had very clear opinions on the matter. People's aesthetics were bruised by the statue. "General" Thompson had a strategy. At some point during the long aftermath of the disappointing boxing match, a guerilla action was proposed.

A team was assembled—an elite group of mature, intelligent adults who all continued to harbor preadolescent cravings to commit acts of petty vandalism. Carter provided the tools and raw materials. On the evening of the raid, the crew traveled to Owl Farm to collect General Thompson. Hunter was nowhere to be found. We'll never know where he really was that evening. Some are sure the raid simply slipped his mind. Others suggest that, during the time between conception and execution, he had been studying obscure texts on military strategy, highlighting passages involving the vast difference between the officer corps and the cannon fodder—and pondering his desire to remain part of the first group. That night the cannon fodder had no choice but to go ahead without their leader. Wheels were turning. The raid was unstoppable.

The sun rose bright and clear the next morning on a proud, rearing zebra. The crime made the front page of the *Aspen Times*. General Hunter called the cannon fodder and congratulated the team on a "righteous mission," with extra points for creativity.

In truth, Hunter was often a no-show. He obeyed only his own laws in life, but the laws of physics are immutable. The inertia of rest was often the most compelling force in his day. Sometimes it could prove impossible to get out of the kitchen.

DICK AND DOC MOVE WEST

By the mid-eighties, Carter was living in the Bay Area and Hunter was writing for the *San Francisco Examiner*. Doc was writing a weekly column and staying in Sausalito; Dick was painting in a garage studio near Redwood City. There would be late-night phone calls while they were both working. Hunter was always nocturnal; Dick could be when he was engrossed in his work.

During that period, *Playboy* magazine assigned Hunter to do a story on porn. As part of this agonizing duty, he was given the job of night manager of the O'Farrell Theater, a one-of-a-kind porn palace run by the Mitchell brothers.

The Mitchell brothers were pioneers in their field. They had discovered legend Marilyn Chambers and had produced such film classics as *Behind the Green Door* and Ms. Chambers's *Insatiable* series. The boys thought the world of Hunter. They had given him a beautiful nickel-plated, high-tech pellet gun. The gun had inscribed on it BECAUSE THIS IS THE WORK WE DO, a quote from *The Godfather: Part II*.

Hunter and Carter took that weapon out into Hunter's backyard one day. The guys were plinking. Their target was a small metal lapel pin depicting San Francisco mayor Dianne Feinstein with eight breasts. Feinstein had some issues with the O'Farrell, and the Mitchell boys had the button made in response to her concerns. Hunter had attached the button to the end of a fishing line and dangled the pole over the edge of the deck. With the button swinging in the breeze, Hunter and Carter proceeded to take turns shooting. Suddenly there was screaming from below. Those shots had to land somewhere.

Buy a box of .22-caliber bullets and the warning on the package reads, "Caution: Range 1 Mile." The range of a pellet gun is far less. Just about to the guy's house down the hill. He seemed upset. Hunter immediately identified the situation as a simple misunderstanding between the target shooters, who were guilty of a minor oversight, and a foolish homeowner who had clearly put his house in a bad spot. Never wishing to offend, Hunter denied everything and told the unhappy neighbor to "fuck off."

At this point they quickly decamped for the O'Farrell. Hunter was going to show Dick around. They took two cars, Thompson in his Wagoneer and Carter in his old MGB. They got down to the O'Farrell, and Hunter introduced Carter all around. The joint was pretty much jumping by that hour, with customers and beautiful girls all over the place. It was a sophisticated operation. Many different rooms with all kinds of different porn shows going on more or less simultaneously. Hunter told one of the guys who worked there to make sure Carter got to see everything. So he did. Dick was constantly hit on by these amazing chicks—because that's how these clubs are but also because Hunter had put out the word that Carter was with him. Hunter was going to get a real kick out of this. Carter's most vivid memory was a room with red shag carpeting all around and up over the benches that ran around the walls, and all mirrors above that, and these two beauties going at each other with four of those flashlights with the long extensions, the ones that they use to guide 747s into the gate at the airport. Those flashlights illuminated every orifice and part imaginable.

Beautiful women kept approaching Carter. He knew what they wanted. They hoped they knew what he wanted—and could provide it. It was business. Dick kept declining kind offer after kind offer. "No, thanks. I'm just here with Hunter doing research," he said. The women were relentless. Dick eventually made his way back up to the office to see what Hunter was up to. They had some drinks, snorted some coke, smoked some weed, and played pool. All while appreciating a constant parade of hot, mostly naked, women.

As Robert Frost once wrote, "The woods are lovely dark and deep, / but I have miles to go before I sleep."

Hours later, Hunter handed Carter a vial of cocaine. Carter couldn't seem to locate an implement with which to snort the stuff. Hunter handed him the keys to his Wagoneer as a useful tool. They continued chatting and shooting pool. It was late; the place was closing up. Hunter and one of the guys had to lock the doors and shut down. Dick left first, waving as he passed them. They were closing the metal shutters on the front of the building.

Carter was home in bed, battling his way toward sleep, when the phone rang. It was Hunter. "Carter, you have my car keys, I couldn't get into the car. Had to go back into the theater, had no ride." Holy shit! thought Dick. The keys were indeed in his pocket, where he had put them after doing the coke. Carter apologized with huge sincerity, and offered to head back to the theater with the keys. "NO. NO, don't apologize. You're going into the Drug Hall of Fame! These things happen when you're doing important work. Call me tomorrow." Hunter hung up.

Carter felt like an asshole, but, wow, he was going into the Drug Hall of Fame. The kids would be so proud.

DICKIE GETS HIS GUN

Hunter liked guns; Carter was not a big gun enthusiast. Dick had little affection for Charlton Heston–loving NRA types. He did enjoy target shooting, though. The rest of us shoot at targets so we can get better when it comes time to shoot at things that annoy us. For Dick, shooting at targets was an end unto itself. A curious notion.

Hunter would take Dick out into the backyard of Owl Farm and they would assassinate the old hot water heater, the beer keg, all the debris that Hunter used as targets. Sometimes they'd shoot at little exploding targets—three-inch-square boxes, about half an inch thick, with a small charge in them. Hunter liked a good conflagration. He was proud of being an excellent marksman, so hitting the target was a good thing, but if it could end up looking like Dresden—or Hell—it was that much better. He'd tape the exploding targets to gallon containers of gasoline. One doesn't need to paint a picture.

One's first experience with the exploding target/gallon of gas continuum is always memorable. Carter's was no exception.

One sunny summer afternoon, a bunch of people were at Owl Farm. It was kind of unusual because there was no particular occasion for their presence there, just a pleasant afternoon. Friends with their children, cronies, drinking buddies. It seemed a perfect time to haul out the weaponry, do some shooting—a "kids having fun" sort of day. So, out came the toys. Everyone was either on the deck or gathered around the picnic table that was about fifteen feet from the deck or somewhere in between. The table was littered with firearms and ammo, plastic gallon jugs, and the little targets. Doc had these big gas tanks, like ranches have. He sent someone off to fill the gallon jugs. The shooting had already begun

Those who shot were blasting away with twelve-gauges, .357 magnums, .44 magnums, AK-47s, and whatever else. Not all at once, of course. Responsibly taking turns. The children watched as if it were a fireworks show. When the jugs of gas showed up, the firing was halted. Hunter took one of the jugs, hiked into the field, and placed it on a log that was upended out there, about fifty feet from the table. The little targets had adhesive backing, and he attached one to the jug.

When he got back to the table, he asked Carter to go inside and grab a fire extinguisher from next to the fireplace. When Carter returned, Hunter said, "Okay, if I catch fire, you put me out." Carter's jaw dropped noticeably, and he backed up about ten paces. "No, no. Stand right here next to me," Hunter said.

Carter did some quick calculations in his head and concluded that if he stood right next to Hunter, and Hunter were engulfed in flame, then Carter, too, would be engulfed in flame. Carter explained his theory to Doc and also admonished the mothers who were standing around to take their children someplace pretty far away. Hunter muttered something no one quite got, but the tone was pure disgust. Carter backed up a little farther.

What followed was a textbook example of "Responsible Shooting and Blowing Things Up." Hunter took careful aim, fired, hit the target. There was a huge fireball. It was like war. He spent the next few minutes directing Carter in extinguishing various patches of lawn that had caught fire. Luckily, no people had. Some of the mothers started herding their children toward their cars.

Hunter had a huge inventory of weapons, from the pedestrian to the exotic—mostly the exotic. Carter was particularly fond of a Browning nine-millimeter. It held twelve rounds in the clip, with one more in the chamber. A serviceable weapon. The exotic stuff would be an acquired taste.

Doc wanted a Carter painting, so Dick proposed a trade, and Hunter bit immediately. Art for weaponry. Doc coughed up the gun right then and there, but Dick asked him if he'd hang on to it. Carter had two young children at home, not to mention an extremely level-headed wife, Claudette, who would consider the notion of a handgun in the house worthy of the Bad Idea Hall of Fame. Dick would use the gun only when he was at Hunter's. Done deal.

Years later Hunter and Carter were having lunch at the Tavern. Dick asked Hunter if he could get the gun. The kids were older, Claudette could be reasoned with. This was fine with Hunter. Doc had some calls to make, so he suggested that Dick come up to Owl Farm in twenty minutes. Hunter headed home to make the calls.

Carter had another soda pop and made his way up to the farm. He arrived to find Andy Hall working on some bookcases in the Red Room. The Red Room connected the house proper with the garage. It had large picture windows on the two exterior walls and fire engine–red carpeting. Dick could hear Hunter on the phone in the kitchen, so he started bantering with Andy to give Hunter some privacy. Hunter appeared in the kitchen doorway, cordless phone up to his ear and the Browning in the other hand. Dick was on the opposite side of the room, standing in the door to the garage, about fifteen feet away. In between, Andy was kneeling down, building bookshelves under the picture windows. Hunter was casually chatting away. Just as casually, he raised the gun. Suddenly the room exploded. Rapid fire in a small, enclosed area. Those things are not indoor toys. Shooting from the hip Hunter ripped a series of holes in the picture windows directly above Andy Hall's head. Andy was not amused, not even a bit. Describing Andy's reaction, Carter used the term *apeshit*. Andy was flattened on the fire engine–red carpet, his head covered, screaming with rage. He had served in the military. All of this was terrible etiquette.

Hunter brought the gun up again, and tossed it to Carter. It was like the scene in the film *2001: A Space Odyssey* in which the pre-human throws the bone up in the air, slow-motion. It was a short distance across the room, but it gave Dick enough time to think things like, It holds twelve rounds, how many shots did he fire? Is the safety on? Is it cocked? Let's count the bullet holes. WHAT THE FUCK DO I DO? These questions seemed exquisitely pertinent at the time. Carter caught the gun. It was empty. Hunter was laughing.

There were now seven beautiful spider-webbed bullet holes in the window, so perfect they looked fake. Carter paused to consider his friend Bob Beattie, who lived across the street in the house the bullets were headed for. Should they call over there? If no one answered, maybe peek in the windows, check for bodies? In the end there was no problem; nobody got hurt. Hunter loved the holes; he had glass double-paned around them to preserve them. They lasted quite a while before eventually collapsing.

BOYS! TAKE YOUR TOYS OUTSIDE!

Besides being a painter, Carter did production design. Some film work, but mostly commercials. He often had occasion to deal with special effects, sometimes pyrotechnics. For smoke effects, the pyro guys would use things that looked like eighteen-inch-long sticks of dynamite. They'd produce acres of thick, noxious white smoke. After a project was completed there'd often be leftovers, so Dick had tons of the smoke bombs kicking around. Something made him think that it was a reasonable idea to give Hunter a case of them. As good ideas go, it was kind of like giving a small child a big box of razor blades to play with. Dick knew Hunter would find a use for them. He did.

It turned out to be yet another example of the inappropriate use of an outside toy. A thing designed to envelop acres was set off in a small roadside tavern. Years later the good people of Woody Creek still speak of the event. Dick still feels kind of bad. Especially now that people know who gave Hunter the bombs.

Carter's last conversation with Hunter was around Christmas 2004. Hunter got word that Dick was going to be in the valley for the holidays, and he called him. He asked Carter if he could bring some of those "fabulous smoke bombs. We have to have plenty of bombs to make New Year's Eve happen." Dick said he'd try but he doubted he could get them. Nobody used them anymore; the smoke was too awful to breathe. He made a couple of calls, to no avail. The holidays came and went with no smoke bomb events.

Early in February, Dick was rummaging in his storage shed and found a beer cooler full of the things. He figured he'd be in Aspen in March or April, and he'd surprise Hunter.

But Hunter died and surprised everyone first.

Now Dick Carter regrets waiting. He wrote:

"What the fuck am I gonna do with these things now? An opportunity for great mayhem has been missed. I should have called him and told him that I found these things. Stupid stuff like that would always buoy the guy, and get him excited. He might have waited. . . . Just a dream.

"Hunter was always great to me. Seemed genuinely glad to see you when you came over. Those visits became fewer over the last years as I spent more time in LA and less time in the valley. But it was always a trip to go by and catch up. Last time I went over was last summer, with Claudette. It was late, after dinner in town and he seemed great. Gave me a signed copy of the last book. Very touched by that. He had his usual cigarette, a cigar, a shot of black jack, beer and a glass of Pepto, all going at once. All seemed normal in the universe."

Thinking about Hunter, Carter sums it up with this:

"One of my favorite HST quotes: 'The music business is a cruel and shallow money trench, a long plastic hallway where thieves and pimps run free, and good men die like dogs. There is also a negative side.'"

Hunter and the Hot Veterinarian

Is He Sick Enough to Get Her Attention?

Randi Bolton is the hottest veterinarian around. She's a huge asset to Woody Creek, and naturally she was a welcome guest at Owl Farm. She first met Hunter at an Aspen party fifteen or so years ago. While she was standing around chatting with her future boyfriend, Don McKinnon, Hunter entered the room. Don, wanting to show her off, called Hunter: "Get over here, there's someone I want you to meet. Doc, this is Randi, she's a veterinarian and drives this special vet pickup truck. It keeps the warm drugs warm and the cold drugs cold." Hunter's eyes widened. His reputation had preceded him. Dr. Bolton threw herself into the doorway, blocking it with her arms, "Touch my truck and you die." Clearly the tiny blonde was the tougher of the two, instantly earning Hunter's respect.

McKinnon and Hunter were buddies and had the same friends. Randi was the closest thing to a responsible adult in that circle. She did no drugs, and when out for the evening, she would stop drinking long before reaching the state of consciousness that everyone else was seeking to achieve at the greatest possible speed. When Hunter was buying the next round and Randi opted out, her boyfriend would dismiss it as a "one drink, one drunk" situation. Hunter would praise her. All beautiful women were potentially Hunter's next girlfriend, if he could just figure out how . . .

Early on, Randi was living on top of a hill in an apartment in a house owned by Alan Finkelstein. Finkelstein was based in L.A. but was an Aspen second homeowner, Little Woody Creek, actually. Randi lived in a small unit upstairs. One evening just after returning home from a hard day tending sick horses, Randi heard the sound of a vehicle speeding up the gravel driveway. It was Hunter, almost a caricature of himself: with the Red Shark's top down, fishtailing, a gambler's visor on his shiny pate, a large glass of Chivas in one hand and a cigarette holder clenched between his teeth.

As the sun set and the gravel flew, he screamed for Alan at the top of his lungs. They had been partying night after night for many days and now night was falling once more. Hunter was ready to go. Finkelstein had already gone. He had left for Los Angeles that morning. Just one of many facts of which Hunter was unaware. Having met Hunter only a couple times at that point, Randi was trying to decide whether to be uneasy or something else. She'd never had to put a human being down. Hunter fell out of the Shark and lurched toward her apartment; he moved with little grace, in fact, little motor control, bellowing still. Randi closed the door. It was handmade, far thicker than any door one could purchase, more like something you'd find in a castle. She slid the deadbolt, hand wrought iron as thick as her wrist. Dr. Bolton was safe, but was Hunter?

Randi thought about it and decided to meet Hunter outside, on open ground. Hunter was taken aback when, instead of his party buddy, the little blonde emerged. "I'm sorry, Hunter, but Alan left this morning." Hunter looked down at her and became thoughtful; his demeanor shifted from wild man to avuncular, and a look of genuine concern crossed his face. "Are you all right? Will you be safe here alone?" She assured Hunter that she was quite safe.

From that time on, Randi did feel safer; she had a real friend and potential protector in the neighborhood. If anyone bothered her and she felt they needed to be shot, she knew whom to call.

About a year later Randi gave a month's notice at the failing veterinary hospital she had been associated with. They told her she was done then and there. On her way home she stopped at the Woody Creek post office, which at the time was located right next to the Tavern. Preoccupied, trying to figure out what she was going to do for work next, she heard shouting from the bar. It was Hunter and Mary Grasso; Mary owned the gallery where Hunter showed his "shot art," paint-splattered images created by shooting at containers full of enamel. They wanted Randi to join them. Sliding onto a bar stool, she announced that they were the first to know that she was opening her own practice. The timing of the transition wasn't exactly what she expected, but so be it; there might be a few awkward weeks. Hunter harrumphed, "You can share office space here at the bar, with me." He called for a phone to alert the owners that two doctors would be sharing space at the Tavern. Dr. Bolton graciously declined.

Weeks later, Hunter was in the midst of a creative frenzy and Randi got an urgent call from him: he needed syringes and sixteen-gauge needles. Not knowing about the creative frenzy thing, she leapt to the most unfortunate conclusions. She stopped by Owl Farm, mostly in the hope that she might be able to talk her friend out of whatever depravity he had in mind.

Armed with speeches about medical ethics, her license to practice, and the dangers of drug abuse, she found Hunter out in the yard armed to the teeth. Large sheets of plywood were propped up all around with photographs and posters wall-papered to them. The images on the plywood were violently splattered with paint and riddled with bullet holes. Hunter would fill vials and balloons with enamel paint, tie strings to them, and strategically drape them down over the pictures and then shoot them. The balloons and vials would explode, send-ing paint flying. This "shot art" had been pioneered by his contemporary and friend, author William Burroughs. Hunter needed the syringes to fill the balloons and vials.

Mary Grasso had been selling Hunter's work at her Aspen gallery for very good money. This was the period when Hunter adopted the attitude that "it wasn't art until it was sold," a philosophy that was repugnant to artists like Michael Cleverly, who chronically had more inventory than sales. For Hunter, though, sales were brisk, and lucrative, and art had to be made.

There was no reason for Randi to have put all this together without any background on the process, so she launched into one of her anti-drug speeches. Hunter stopped her and affected a pathetic, hurt expression. How could anyone think that he might do something unseemly with syringes and needles? He explained what he was up to. When Randi looked around, it became obvious, of course; the whole thing was about truth and beauty. She gave him what he asked for.

Randi and Doc were always honest with each other. Randi was always honest with everyone, but some people tended to tell Hunter what they thought he wanted to hear. One night Randi wandered into the Tavern, and there was Hunter holding court with a bunch of acolytes. Randi had always heard of Hunter's famous mumble but had never actually noticed it. That night he was in full garble, with the acolytes nodding and smiling, not necessarily in unison or comprehension. When he saw Randi he greeted her and asked her to join the group, then continued his dissertation, more or less addressing it to her. When he finally paused, Randi said, "Hunter, I can't understand a word you're saying." Hunter smiled, winked at her, and said with perfect diction, "Good for you." With that, he turned back to his audience and proceeded to mumble. His fans got back to nodding and smiling, not necessarily in unison.

Randi later posed sort of in the buff (there was a damn horse standing in front of everything of interest) for *Calendar Vets 2005*, a fund-raiser for Colorado Animal Rescue, Inc. It was a big hit all over and was prominently displayed in Hunter's kitchen. Hunter died in February; the month on the calendar was August, as it had been since the day it was hung on the wall. It was Randi's month.

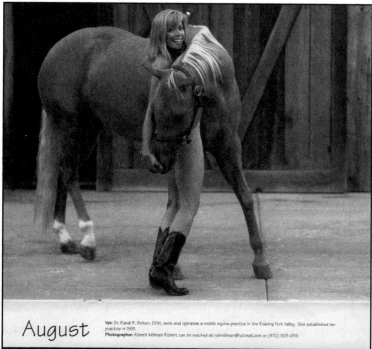

August

Vet: Dr. Ranel R. Bolton, DVM, owns and operates a mobile equine practice in the Roaring Fork Valley. She established her practice in 1991.

Photographer: Robert Millman Robert can be reached at robmillman@hotmail.com or (970) 923-8911.

SUN	MON	TUE	WED	THU	FRI	SAT
	1	2	3	4	5 ●	6
						Puttin' on The Dog and Cat Ball
7	8	9	10	11	12	13 ☽
14	15	16	17	18	19 ○	20
						National Homeless Animal Day
21	22	23	24	25	26 ☾	27
28	29	30	31			

July

					1	2
3	4	5	6	7	8	9
10	11	12	13	14	15	16
17	18	19	20	21	22	23
24	25	26	27	28	29	30

September

				1	2	3
4	5	6	7	8	9	10
11	12	13	14	15	16	17
18	19	20	21	22	23	24
25	26	27	28	29	30	

A Cowboy Helps Hunter Out, Again and Again and Again

Jesse Steindler was the manager of the Flying Dog Ranch, three miles up Woody Creek Road from Owl Farm. By rural Woody Creek standards, that made him a fairly close neighbor of Hunter's. This was not always a big plus in Jesse's mind.

Jesse had been a working cowboy from the age of sixteen. He considered his horse and big hat about as glamorous as a carpenter would consider his hammer and saw. When, on occasion, someone asked him if he wanted to go riding, he'd respond that "riding a horse for fun would be like going for a ride in a wheelbarrow." Like most real cowboys, Jesse didn't set aside too much of his day for nonsense.

Jesse and his family took up residence at the Flying Dog in the early nineties. It was Jesse, his first wife, their twin toddler boys, and daughters Julia, eight, and Alice, ten. Jesse had heard about the eccentric celebrity who lived down the road. One afternoon he stopped by Owl Farm to introduce himself and to alert Hunter to the fact that he was moving 150 head of cattle down from the ranch to the pasture directly across from Owl Farm the following morning. Hunter thought this was great and indicated that he would be around to videotape the event.

Shortly after dawn, Jesse and his daughters started moving the herd. Jesse up front, and the two girls in the rear. They grazed them down the road, moving slowly, with the animals stopping at every curve and bend so their buddies in the rear could catch up. This was in the last days before the rich started building in Woody Creek, so there was little traffic to be inconvenienced by a herd of cattle at that hour. The herd was about 150 yards from Hunter's house when Jesse saw Hunter out on his deck. He noticed that Hunter had a gun. Jesse was too busy with the cows, each one with ideas of its own, to think much about it. They were directly opposite Owl Farm and beginning to try to turn the herd into the pasture when Hunter opened fire.

Jesse was acquainted with a number of Hunter Thompson stories; some of them featured firearms. His first thought was that Hunter was shooting at them. Of course Doc would never do that; he was pointing the weapon in the opposite direction, toward the mesa behind the house. Jesse figured this out pretty quick, but the cows didn't. It was too fine a detail for their bovine brains to distinguish. The herd exploded like a flock of birds, with 150 cows taking off at full gallop in 150 different directions. Hunter blasted off half a dozen rounds while Jesse and his daughters tried to keep from getting trampled. They watched helplessly as the beasts charged back up the road where they had come from, down the road toward the Woody Creek Tavern, up through Hunter's yard toward the mesa beyond, and off in every other available direction. Jesse was getting to know Hunter, and his sense of humor.

It took Jesse and his girls two hours to round up the cattle and get them into the pasture. Being ranch folk, they didn't think it was quite as big a deal as some might have, but Jesse felt he should have a little chat with Doc nonetheless. New in the neighborhood and new to the job, he didn't think it was his place to be overly critical of Hunter's behavior. They had a quiet talk and, with the benefit of perspective, Jesse came to think it was pretty funny, too. Hunter had just wanted to see what would happen. Living across from Owl Farm, the critters were going to be exposed to a lot of gunfire; they might as well start getting used to it.

Soon Jesse and Hunter became friends. Jesse was a good neighbor to everyone and was always willing to lend a hand. He was as capable at standard household repairs as Hunter was not. When the godawful pink toilet sprang a leak, and Hunter apparently thought it was the sort of thing that could be repaired with a baseball bat, Deborah could make an urgent call to Jesse and he'd come over, turn the water off, and install a new toilet. Standing in water up to his ankles, he'd only ask that Hunter do his yelling in the other room. There was no waiting to be fit into a plumber's schedule or need to frighten an outsider. When the official Owl Farm skunk, varmint, and predator trapper finally had enough of Hunter and quit, Jesse took over those duties, too. He used smaller traps so the skunks couldn't lift their tails and spray. He never complained—but damn those 3:00 or 4:00 A.M. phone calls.

By the summer following Hunter's "recreational stampede," Jesse had been at the ranch for a year, and everyone understood one another. They weren't grazing cattle across from Owl Farm anymore; they were growing hay. Hay has no response to gunfire. It was approximately 3:00 A.M. one fine day when Jesse's phone rang. Hunter's newest "editorial assistant" was on the line. Hunter was stuck in the hayfield. Those of us who have driven out of the Owl Farm driveway countless times always thought we had two options, left and right. Hunter had discovered option three: straight. He, the assistant, and the old Jeep Cherokee had bounced a hundred yards down into the field. Hay requires an awful lot of water, and therfore a lot of irrigating. The field was being irrigated that night and was really, really wet. Hunter had buried the Jeep up to the axles. The hay was three feet high, which rendered the Jeep, and Hunter, almost totally invisible. The assistant left Hunter in and bushwhacked back up to the house to call Jesse, who dutifully got up and headed to Owl Farm.

When he arrived, the assistant refused to leave the house. Hunter's mood was too foul, and she wanted no part of whatever was going to happen next. Jesse got into the old ranch pickup he was driving and set out into the field to find Doc. Since Jesse was the one who did the irrigating, he knew where to drive and where not to. He kept to the fence line, the dry ground. Circumnavigating the field, he finally spotted Hunter's Jeep, only because of the flash of a lighter and the glow of a pipe in the interior. The roof was the only thing visible above the hay. Jesse turned off his rig and approached. He tapped his flashlight on Hunter's driver's-side window, in the style of a cop rousting teenagers at play. Hunter jolted and locked the doors. Clearly the flashlight tap had called up some disturbing, primal memory, some situation that he did not want to revisit. He hunkered down, pretending not to exist.

Hunter had bogged himself down in the worst possible place. The giant agricultural sprinklers used to water a hay field are pretty much the same as the back-and-forth oscillating type that you use on your lawn, only much, much bigger. Each one covered about an acre, with the maximum amount of water being dumped at the outside of the arc. In this case, approximately twenty gallons of water were being dumped on Hunter's Jeep every thirty seconds. The water was cycling back toward the Jeep, and Jesse really wanted to get inside. Hunter had been sitting in there smoking hash since the assistant had left and was feeling a little paranoid. There was a sense of urgency. Jesse finally shined the flashlight into his own semi-panicky face so Hunter could recognize him. Hunter unlocked a door.

So now it was 4:00 A.M. and Hunter and the cowboy were filling the Jeep with hash smoke, and water was pounding down on the roof every thirty seconds. Jesse had to be up to run a ranch in a couple of hours and really wanted this to be over. Of course at this point, he was completely stoned.

Through the smoke, Jesse could see that just out beyond the arc of the sprinkler was dry ground. He reckoned that if he could get his ranch truck to the point closest to Hunter, an area that was still dry, he might have enough purchase to be able to drag the Jeep out. He timed his break between drenchings and made for the truck. He brought the rig up as close to the Jeep as he dared and stretched out the tow strap; it was just short. Rummaging around the bed, he found some old rope with which to make up the distance. He triple-wrapped the rope between the hook on the tow strap and the truck's undercarriage. Jesse and Hunter conferred, made a plan, and got to work. Soon they were behind the wheels of the two vehicles, tires spinning wildly, mud and hay flying, rope straining. Well, the strap held, but the rope broke. Under the strain, it snapped like a rubber band, and the steel hook flew back over the Jeep's hood and shattered the windshield. Hunter came flying out of the Jeep as if he'd been shot from a cannon. For some reason he was sure it was a bullet. Pure paranoia. The timing wasn't good. Hunter flattened himself on the ground, to present a smaller target to the phantom sniper, just as the sprinkler arrived depositing its twenty-gallon load. Hunter, usually as capable of appreciating low comedy as much as anybody, was having a little trouble with this one.

Jesse drove the soaked and livid Hunter S. Thompson home. As Hunter sloshed out of the truck, he screamed at Jesse to never call him again. Jesse could have let it go, but he had a better handle on the humor of the situation than Hunter. He reminded Doc who actually had done the calling at 3:00 A.M. The conversation ended right there.

It was after 1:00 A.M. Christmas morning. Jesse had finished wrapping presents at midnight and had made it to bed to try to get a couple in before the kids got up. The phone rang. Jesse's wife, Jill, answered. It was Deborah. "There's a mountain lion in the house!" Jill handed the phone to Jesse.

"Ha ha," Jesse said. He could hear Hunter in the background; they were on the speakerphone. Considering the holiday, Jesse just assumed that Hunter was giving the gift of "mirth" for Christmas this year.

Hunter came on:

"Jesuschristthisisnofuckingjokethere'sagoddamnmountain lioninthegoddamnhousewillyougetoverhere?"

Jesse patiently suggested that mountain lions were more the bailiwick of the Fish and Game Department, and perhaps that's who they should be calling at two-something o'clock on Christmas morning. Jesse was pretty sure that Hunter and Deborah wouldn't have any luck with Fish and Game, but he figured that if Hunter was screaming at their answering machine then he wouldn't be hollering at him. It might buy him enough time to take a ball-peen to every phone in the house and become incommunicado. This, of course, didn't play, and Jesse found himself hiking it up Hunter's steps, .30-30 in hand, not too many minutes later. As it turned out the critter, whatever it was, wasn't in the house. It was in the peacock cage.

The peacock cage was on the deck built up against the house. Five or six feet square and about eight feet high. It was cobbled together with two-bys, chicken wire, and Plexiglas. On the deck side was a person-size door made out of chicken wire and two-bys. On the opposite wall was a smaller peacock-size door. Inside were shelves and perches running up two walls. Apparently peacocks like banana peels and orange rinds and stuff of that nature, so between cleanings, the interior of the cage looked like a compost heap covered with bird shit.

© Chloe Sells

The peacock cage, sans mountain lion, bobcat, lynx . . . whatever.

Jesse was plenty nervous when he started easing the cage door open. He noticed that Hunter was standing behind him with a shotgun. Jesse pleaded with him to go somewhere else. He didn't want it to turn into a shooting gallery. He peered in; the birds were all huddled together on a top perch. He looked to his right and realized he was nose to nose with an extremely large, agitated bobcat. Backing up slowly, he left the door wide open.

The cat's butt was pressed up against the chicken wire. Jesse figured that if he gave him a poke with the barrel of the .30-30, the frightened cat would run out the open door and be gone. Jesse poked; the cat hissed. Kind of like a house cat, only basso profundo. It was a toss-up as to who was more anxious, Jesse or the cornered cat. Jesse poked again, harder. The cat sprang, bounced off a window, hit the floor running, out the cage door and in through the living room door where Hunter had been standing. Now there really was a wildcat in the house.

The decor of Hunter's house was what you'd call eclectic. A little cluttered in some areas. There must have been a million places for a cat to hide, half a million in the living room alone. The stuffed wolverine, the skulls, the gator heads. This wasn't going to be easy. The two intrepid hunters stood in the middle of the room peering and pointing the barrels of their guns in this direction and that. No bobcat to be seen. They flung the front door open all the way and decided to open all the windows to make it easier for the cat to escape. After opening the last window as far as they could, they turned back to the search. Suddenly they heard a sound behind them and spun around. It wasn't the cat. It was the last window they had opened. It was newly installed; the carpenter had set it in the rough opening, but hadn't yet nailed it in place. This sort of thing wasn't totally uncommon at Owl Farm. Sometimes workers would feel the need to leave in a hurry; sometimes they'd ingest something that would leave them confused. Jesse and Hunter watched, paralyzed, as the window, frame and all, slowly tilted in, crashed onto the living room floor, and shattered. It was December 25. Hunter's house was becoming pretty chilly. Snow was flurrying in through the huge new hole in the wall.

The good news was that the crash had frightened the cat, too. Driven from its hiding place, it sat perched on the back of an easy chair. Jesse had had enough. He raised his rifle. The bullet went through the bobcat, the wall behind the bobcat, Hunter's bedroom, and into the back wall of the house. Later Hunter never let anyone dig it out or patch it. He liked having stuff around to remind him of the good times.

One summer a few years later, the phone company was trenching along the side of Woody Creek Road, burying fiber optic lines. It was a long project, and Jesse had befriended the guys working on it. He might have thought twice about doing this, though, if he had known that it would mean he'd become the unofficial liaison between the crew and the neighborhood. Specifically, Hunter.

One day, when they'd trenched their way fairly close to Owl Farm, Jesse hooked up with the guys after work. He pointed out that there was a lot of stuff buried under Hunter's driveway: electric conduits, security gear, and more. There was also a large water line that came down from the Salvation Ditch behind Hunter's, crossed under the road, and provided irrigation water for the hay field (the one Hunter didn't drive around in anymore). The 8-inch line carried water under about 143 pounds of pressure. At the time, it seemed that the boys had taken due note of these facts. Unfortunately these guys were enjoying all that Aspen could offer, partywise. It was a rare treat for their work to bring them so close to a sexy resort town, so they tended to show up for work a little hungover.

Jesse's helpful tips apparently slipped their collective mind. When they hit the water main, it blew the trenching machine clear out of its trench. The geyser was forty feet high. People could easily have been killed. Eventually, replacing the pipe was going to require digging a ditch thirty feet long, fifteen feet wide, and seven or eight feet deep. Fortunately, the force of all that water had created a sinkhole almost that size. Unfortunately, that sinkhole was formerly known as Hunter's driveway.

The event roused Hunter from his slumber.

Jesse got wind of the crisis and rushed to Owl Farm. He headed up to the ditch and turned the water off.

Normally Hunter could go days without leaving the farm. He could go days without looking out the window. The fact that it was now utterly impossible to get a vehicle out of the driveway made for a new, urgent, desire to go for a spin. He swelled to twice his normal size with righteous indignation. He set Deborah to alerting the media, his attorneys, and the police—in that order. She did this, and they all showed up.

Hunter's house is on a narrow bend on Woody Creek Road. All these people, plus the work crew, converging at the same time created their own traffic jam. Possibly the first in Woody Creek history, if you don't count cows. It was chaos: with Hunter yelling, reporters reporting, photographers photographing, cops taking statements, lawyers computing billable hours, and trenching crew skulking and sulking.

Since Jesse was the only one who had any kind of rapport with the crew, in Hunter's mind, this was all his fault. What was he going to do about it? Hunter was frothing. He wanted blood. Heads must roll. Things were becoming unpleasant. There was no question there'd been a mistake, and no small one. Hunter had pointed this out, and continued to do so. The crew was freaked out; they were in deep shit and it was getting deeper. It was a good gig and they were in serious danger of losing their jobs, plus there was the matter of whatever happened next. What happened next could be a lot worse than mere unemployment. Hunter's behavior was making that clear.

Eventually, Jesse couldn't take it anymore. At the closest possible range, he reminded Hunter that Hunter Thompson was traditionally and famously a champion of the little guy, and that his insistence on tacking these fellas up on crosses wasn't consistent with that policy and that maybe he could back off just a little bit. Hunter actually listened to reason. The repairs took the rest of that day and all the next. Hunter was nowhere to be seen.

The crew was understandably eager to put Owl Farm behind them. With the driveway repairs complete, they continued trenching along in front of the Owl Farm yard. They still had a way to go before Hunter was a thing of the past. Between the crew and Hunter was Hunter's split-rail fence. Behind that was the long row of cordwood, which acted as another fence, and behind that, a row of beautiful cottonwoods. It seemed like sufficient insulation.

The work crew reached and passed Hunter's property line on a typically pleasant Woody Creek summer afternoon. Surely there was a lot of relief going around. A nice little wind kicked up. Deborah was on the deck when the first cottonwood came down. When it hit the lawn, the uppermost branches were eight feet from the deck. Deborah was rooted to the spot; the trees weren't. A second tree came down. Deborah's mouth hung open, frozen with fear. A third toppled. The crew had trenched right through their root systems and the trees were just standing there waiting for a stiff breeze.

Deborah had been with Hunter long enough to pick up a few of his personality traits. Hence, she wasn't given to understatement. Hunter's slumber was once again disturbed.

Neither Jesse Steindler nor God Almighty could chill Hunter out this time. "There's one other thing about little people: they shouldn't be incompetent" was the phrase that echoed in Jesse's ears for some time to come.

The phone company bought Hunter not three but six lovely new cottonwoods. Along with the trees, they sent a crew of non-English-speaking Latinos to plant them, the idea being to keep verbal intercourse between the workers and the home-owner to a minimum. Hunter watched them like a hawk. He didn't sleep, probably didn't eat. His interest was so up close and personal that the laborers, even without language skills or knowing the history of the situation, were getting edgy. The idea of the workers not speaking the language was a good one from the phone company's point of view, but not great for Jesse. Hunter had things to say and he wanted them under-stood. Jesse spoke Spanish, so he was once again in the middle. Deborah was constantly on the phone to him to come over to translate for Hunter. Once the Latinos got a load of what was on Hunter's mind, and saw the inventory of weapons that he was sporting when he came out on the deck to glare at them, they worked in a state of abject terror.

They finished the project in record time and did a fine job. The feeling in the neighborhood was that the Latinos' next move would be to make a break across the border . . . straight back to Mexico.

When the temperature of the indoor pool at the Flying Dog Ranch wasn't to Hunter's liking, Hunter would call Jesse. Jesse had nothing to do with the pool.

When Hunter's car wouldn't start, he'd call Jesse. Jesse was good with machinery, but his job description at the ranch was "cowboy." He suggested that Hunter call him when his horse wouldn't start.

Hunter would take Jesse's girls on high-speed convertible rides in the Shark. The girls were growing up hot. Jesse would ask where they were and be told that Hunter had taken them for a ride. He'd wring his hands and be unable to concentrate until they were returned. They'd come back full of McDonald's, bearing souvenirs autographed by Doc, making statements like "Gee, I've never driven so fast in a car. I thought Julia was going to blow right out of the backseat!"

Hunter placed a high value on Jesse's friendship. Of all the skills that Jesse possessed, the one that Hunter valued most was his talent and creativity with explosives. Anyone can speak Spanish or get a car started, but blowing the crap out of stuff—now that was something special.

The boys got an inner tube from the tire off a John Deere 966 loader. The tire on that loader is about five feet high. When you take the tube out and inflate it, without the tire to contain the thing, it can swell beyond all expectation. The guys were counting on this because they were going to fill the tube with acetylene, which they did. A risky and technically demanding process, it involved hoses that had to be flushed with water afterward and a total absence of combustibles. Once inflated, the tube was huge, a giant black doughnut eight feet across and four feet high, full of acetylene. Acetylene requires an open flame to ignite. They duct-taped a dynamite fuse to the tire, which would burn down and when it got to the tire, would melt the rubber and. . .

An enthusiastic crowd gathered at Owl Farm for the event; this was to be a first. No one knew what would happen. No one had even heard of this sort of thing being attempted before. Jesse lit the fuse before the assembled congregation of conflagration aficionados. He had used four feet of fuse to make sure that he had sufficient time to get a safe distance away. Nonetheless, it took all his willpower to turn his back and walk away. Every fiber of his being said run.

Jesse joined the crowd and watched the fuse. It burned slowly, and the audience, as one, inched farther back as the seconds passed. When the fuse disappeared under the tire, they waited. It seemed like long seconds were passing. They began craning, jockeying for position, slowly inching closer.

One of the gang was running late. He was four miles away when he saw a massive orange glow in the sky. Then the concussion hit him; he felt it even though he was in his car.

Back at Owl Farm everyone was flat on their backs. It was beautiful, a fierce orange-pink glow rising fifty feet into the air. No smoke, just the glow rising straight up, and incredible heat. The bottom half of the tube was melted into the lawn in a scorched circle.

Nobody got hurt. The only one who counted the broken windows at Owl Farm was the guy who fixed them.

Growing Up Across the Street from Hunter

THE FREEDOM TRACTOR

Zeno Beattie is the son of Bob Beattie, sports commentator and former U.S. Olympic ski team coach. The Beatties moved to Woody Creek in 1976, the year Claudine Longet, singer, actress, and ex-wife of crooner Andy Williams, shot Spider Sabich, former Olympic skier and well-liked local. The murder was national news, and Beattie had been very close to the victim. Woody Creek seemed peaceful compared to what had been going on in Aspen.

Zeno was raised across the street, a stone's throw from Owl Farm. He grew up with a love of the outdoors, including hunting. Zeno and Hunter shared a common appreciation of firearms, though to different purpose (if it can be said that Hunter's love of firearms had purpose). They were buddies from the get-go, and as Zeno got older he became increasingly helpful to Hunter around the farm, usually with guy stuff, tractor stuff.

At one point early on, what used to be Hunter's two cabins and acreage became a farm, "Owl Farm." If his spread was a farm, then Hunter was a farmer, a gentleman farmer of course. As this idea took hold and grew in his mind, he began to think about the accouterments of farming and began to lust for a tractor. Zeno and his dad had purchased a John Deere

Bob Beattie, Zeno, and Zeno's boys, R.A. and Ben.

in 1983. The John Deere became the object of Hunter's desire, and it was just across the street. Hunter could see it, he could taste it. The idea of Hunter's needing a tractor wasn't totally frivolous. Doc had a lot of yard to mow, and sometimes things, once blown up, needed to be buried. Sneaking a backhoe up to Owl Farm to bury evidence wasn't always convenient or easy; having a tractor on hand could make stealth disposal a relative snap. There are

entire motor vehicles buried on Owl Farm. As far as I know, none is occupied.

The "Shark" waiting for summer.

In the mid-eighties, Hunter had a little dustup with a porn actress that had him facing criminal charges in Pitkin County. It was serious stuff: assault, drugs, weapons, nothing to joke about.

BEWARE

Today: the Doctor
Tomorrow: You

The Hunter S. Thompson Legal Defense Fund
Box 274, Woody Creek, Colorado 81656

© Chloe Sells

Reflecting Hunter's sense of persecution at the hands of the authorities.

Hunter had been researching porn for a magazine article. Ultimately that research evolved into a book that never happened, but it was the research that counted. Fortunately for Woody Creek, the research involved women who were part of that industry flying into Aspen to be interviewed by Doc. They'd make their way to the Tavern from the airport and the bartender would call Hunter to clear them, make sure they were invited guests. Hunter would come down and pick them up, but not until they'd cooled their heels for an hour or so. This was Hunter's little gift to the boys at the bar. Usually things went fine; you can write that scenario yourself. On this one occasion it was different. The young lady in question exited Owl Farm screaming, and the authorities were called. Some said there was an incident in the hot tub. The thing went to court, the broad got a case of amnesia, and the case was dismissed, but not before Doc and his circle experienced a long period of intense anxiety. Hunter and everyone who cared for him were euphoric about the dismissal of the case, and there was to be a huge celebration at Owl Farm. Hunter called Zeno from the courthouse steps. "Get me a tractor!" It was Hunter's victory treat to himself. Zeno told Hunter he'd start looking into it the very next day. "No, I want it now, today!" "Are you planning to pay for it?" Zeno asked.

Zeno had done business with a tractor/farm implement dealership in Grand Junction and was on pretty good terms with them. He called his guy, Marv, and told him that Hunter needed a tractor just like his. Marv was predictably pleased; it was an easy sale. Then Zeno told him that it had to be delivered that day. This was a different story. Same-day delivery service for tractors isn't as common as you might think. After a great deal of dickering and wheedling, Marv agreed to load the thing up and bring it to Woody Creek. He made the 125-mile trip from Junction, and Zeno met him at the Tavern to guide him up to Owl Farm. When they got there, the party was in full swing, and it wasn't a Grand Junction sort of party. Things were taking place that Marv probably wasn't used to. He and Zeno unloaded the tractor, and Zeno left a nervous Marv to search for Hunter and get a check.

He first ran into Hunter's trusted friend Michael Solheim, who was functioning as Doc's business manager/check writer at the time. Michael had heard nothing of this tractor business and said there was no way he was cutting a huge check. "Hunter has no money. Load it up and take it back to Junction," he said. Hunter appeared, and the argument began. Ten minutes later, he came walking out of the house with a check for Marv, and the John Deere became "the Freedom Tractor," to commemorate Hunter's not going to jail for doing something disgusting and illegal to a porn actress.

Hunter was thrilled with his new toy. Zeno gave him a quick course in Tractor 101: shifting, working the mower attachment, finding where the fuel goes. Doc was always good with machinery and was a quick study. He started the tractor up and off he went, mowing away in no discernable pattern, back, forth, circles, across, with partygoers scrambling to avoid the mower blades that could be coming at them from any direction at any time, all this at high speed, bouncing through areas of rocks, wire, and debris that had never before seen a blade. When Hunter tired of it, he just parked his prize in the middle of the front lawn.

Hunter's beloved tractor, Jesse Steindler, and Doc's personal film biographer, Wayne Ewing.

There the Freedom Tractor sat. After a month, Zeno couldn't stand it any longer and decided to finish the mowing job. Obviously the lawn was more than ready, and he thought he might set a good example. He had wisely kept a spare key, assuming that

Hunter was bound to lose his. He jumped on and started mowing, round and round, in an orderly professional pattern. A few laps into the project Doc came screaming out of the house spewing obscenities and waving his favorite nickel-plated machine gun. He was wearing purple sunglasses, so Zeno couldn't see his eyes. "Who'sfuckingwithmytractor?" Zeno considered diving off the thing but instead hunkered down low, next to the steering wheel, and waved, hoping to be recognized. "Ohuhit'syouZeno." Hunter's sputtering was winding down. "Just thought I'd do some mowing," Zeno called from behind the wheel. "Gooduh. Lookslikeitneedsit." Zeno finished the lawn, and Hunter retired to the kitchen.

Hunter adored his tractor. He'd drive it around with no real purpose in mind. Once a month he'd have Zeno come over and they'd change the oil and do whatever other maintenance was deemed necessary. One of these occasions was prefaced by a phone call from Hunter suggesting that he "wasn't sure" if the tractor was running. "What do you mean? You're not sure if the tractor will start?" Zeno asked. He made his way across the street to Owl Farm and started the tractor with no problem. He then shut it off and proceeded to drain the oil. While the oil was draining he began a general survey and . . . "HUNTER, WHY DID YOU SHOOT YOUR TRACTOR?" The hole in the fuel tank was unmistakably that of the "bullet" variety. Hunter denied everything; he would never do such a thing. "You're goddamn lucky it's a diesel. If it were gas it would have blown up!" Hunter once again denied any knowledge of tractors and bullets and started sputtering about searching for the culprit. It was a simple welding project for Zeno to patch the hole; Hunter's job was to track down the sniper. Zeno had the greater success.

THE INTERVIEW

The following winter, the World Cup ski racers were in Aspen. It was a big deal; Aspen has always coveted these premier ski events. The races were sponsored by Subaru and were being covered by ESPN. This meant that Zeno's dad, Bob, who had a long association with both companies, would be doing the TV commentary. Also on the TV team was announcer/commentator Andrea Joyce. Joyce would later marry anchorman Harry Smith. While Bob Beattie was to report the races as they happened, Joyce's job was to prerecord "color" pieces about Aspen and other things of interest. She decided that a piece on Woody Creek's famous Hunter S. Thompson would be fun. She knew that Bob was Hunter's neighbor and asked if he could set things up with Hunter. Bob thought it was a very bad idea. He refused, trying to explain that he knew Hunter, and she didn't, and that she'd just have to take his word. This of course piqued her interest even more, so she asked Zeno if he could speak to Hunter on her behalf. Of course Zeno also knew it was a bad idea, but being young and frisky, he figured it could be pretty damn funny, too. "Sure, I'll ask Hunter," he said.

At first Hunter didn't want anything to do with it, but Zeno convinced him that it might be good for business. He could reach a whole different audience: people who watch ski racing on TV. Hunter eventually acquiesced. Zeno made arrangements to meet Joyce and her camera crew at the Aspen Airport liquor store. At the store, Zeno outfitted them with the largest bottles he could find of all of Hunter's favorites; it was a lot of booze. Off they went to Owl Farm.

The little band arrived. Hunter greeted them and ushered the eager group inside. After a quick tour it was determined that they'd set up in the living room. Hunter and Zeno retired to the kitchen while Joyce supervised the setting up of the cameras and sound equipment. This event happened to coincide with a period of time when Hunter had actually bugged his own house. He had microphones in all the rooms and speakers by his stool at the kitchen counter. Hunter and Zeno listened to every word that was said during the setting-up process. I guess you could say that at times Hunter could be a weasel in the purest sense of the word. It was, however, entertaining as hell. When one of the crew would come into the kitchen to announce that they were ready, Hunter would stall, say he wasn't ready, and he and Zeno would go back to eavesdropping and giggling at the grumbling and moaning that was going on in the living room. The crew was kept waiting for a very long time. Then, when it was clear that everyone was right at the breaking point, Hunter decided he was ready.

Zeno recalls that it was a great interview, and that it actually made the telecast. Andrea Joyce had obviously done her homework and was knowledgeable about a broad range of things "Hunter Thompson." She asked a lot of great questions and finally came to the guns. "What's the deal with the guns?" she asked. Hunter reached under the couch, pulled out the nickel-plated machine gun, and in the same motion, pulled back the slide. "Is that thing loaded?" a number of people asked all at once. The atmosphere had changed instantly, and *nervous* would be the word to describe it. Hunter threw open the front door, stepped out onto the deck, and let rip until the weapon was empty.

You might be surprised how many people could lead their whole lives without ever hearing the sound of a submachine gun being fired at close range. Judging from the reaction, some of those people were at Hunter's that evening.

Expensive equipment that had taken an hour-plus to set up was literally thrown into their rental car. Five minutes later the crew was packed up and heading out the driveway, trailing cords and random bits of high-tech equipment.

Andrea Joyce was left to ponder which of the Beattie men had been right. Sure, she got her interview, but was it a good idea?

A Lawyer Learns from an Expert

Mick Ireland was a Pitkin County commissioner; he was also a lawyer. Before that he was a reporter for the *Aspen Times*. As a politician, he was to the left, pretty far. As a human being he was pretty conservative. He didn't smoke, drink, or do drugs. He seemed to enjoy eating, but you'd never know it to look at him. He was as lean as they come. Probably because he rode his goddamn bicycle about a million miles a week.

It could be said that Mick spent his political career pissing people off. Particularly rich people. His enemies tried to recall him on three occasions. Their efforts never succeeded. Each time Mick ran for office, a group of wealthy conservatives threw piles of money at the opposing candidate. Always anonymously. Mick would win, and they'd throw piles of money at a recall effort. Always anonymously. And they would fail. Always anonymously. Why were they so upset? Mick could be direct, abrupt—okay, rude sometimes. Regular people are used to rudeness; we get it all the time, we're inured to it. The wealthy aren't; it hurts their feelings, or whatever they have in there.

Mick first came to Hunter's attention in the early seventies. A local rancher thought that he would solve Aspen's housing problems by making himself incredibly rich. The guy really wasn't fooling anyone, but in those days people, and the newspaper, leaned toward civility. Mick wrote a scathing column for the *Aspen Times* in which he compared the rancher to Nixon and his "secret plan," and in general vilified the guy three ways to Sunday. Hunter approved. From then on, even though it would be years before Mick sought office, Hunter knew that he had a political ally.

In the mid-eighties Mick was still reporting for the *Aspen Times*. A local "import/export" guy with what seemed to be excellent Bolivian connections had just finished a couple sets of tennis at a fancy local club. Someone had carelessly left a pipe bomb on the undercarriage of his Jeep directly beneath the driver's seat. When he started it up, he was blown to smithereens. This was a big deal for Aspen. That sort of thing never happened. It made people think.

One thing that people thought about was how many of their friends were either in rehab or jail. What they concluded (some of them) was that maybe drugs weren't good for you. Mick had always been of that opinion. During the course of the police investigation, Mick got hold of the smithereens guy's papers, which included a lot of names, and published fifty-four of them. The implication was that these people were in the import/export business, too. For a small town like Aspen, this was a big scandal. It was also the kind of behavior that would get you on Hunter's shit list till the end of time. To his credit Hunter never held it against Mick. He understood that he and Mick had fundamental disagreements regarding their respective hobbies, and they basically agreed to disagree. Mick was doing what he thought was right, no matter how much Doc disapproved of the concept of outing small businessmen.

It wasn't long after that Mick decided to go to law school. He figured he'd become a lawyer instead of just creating all these clients for other people. . . .

By 3:00 A.M. on a Monday in August 1987, Mick was a law student living in a Boulder apartment with no air-conditioning. It was hot. When the phone rang he wasn't thinking "party." "Hi, is Mick there?" asked a cheery female voice in tones better suited to the middle of the day. Mick quelled his instincts, the sarcastic ones, and admitted to being himself. "Yes, how may I help you?" "I need some beer" was the cheerful response. Of all the people in Boulder, Mick was the last person to be likely to have beer kicking around at 3:00 A.M. He didn't use it. He biked, he ran, he went to class, and he slept whenever he could. Three o'clock in the morning had always seemed like a great time for the sleeping part.

But, as fate would have it, Mick actually did have some beer in the wee hours of that summer morning. He had recently hosted a party for new law students whom he'd been tutoring and there were leftovers. "Who is this?" he asked. "Kathy. You know, Kathy. Hunter's wife," she said. People's wives don't generally call Mick at that hour—and Hunter? The only "Hunter" that Mick could think of was, well, Hunter. But it didn't make any sense to Mick. And he didn't know anything about any Kathy.

Kathy explained that Hunter was in town and couldn't write his column without beer. She acted as if she and Mick had been buddies for years and the request couldn't be more ordinary. Mick asked the same question that so many of Hunter's friends have asked themselves on so many occasions over so many years. "Why me?"

Kathy explained that the beer had to be delivered to a motel in Boulder so Hunter Thompson could write. Mick was inclined to accommodate. He had enrolled Dr. Thompson in the CU class of 1988 by adding his name to the seating charts circulated by the less-than-hip professorate. The joy of hearing a professor address a fellow student as "Mr. Thompson" and ask for the holding in some obscure law case lingered.

Mick shook his next ex-girlfriend awake. He offered her the chance to meet the famous celebrity, author, political junkie. By his own admission, the lady in question, Eileen, was smarter than he. She practiced law in areas whose boundaries Mick was soon likely to cross. She didn't fancy junkies of any kind, including political ones. She declined. Mick had a difficult time understanding. The chance to deliver beer to a degenerate in a seedy hotel at three in the morning? What's not to like? She might get to watch him write something. Eileen stuck with "no."

Mick soon found himself wandering down hallways carpeted in mildew red and accented with duct tape and lit by fluorescent lights. The air-conditioning rumbled and wheezed ineffectually in the background. A little bit of real America, with the new center for creative writing in Boulder serving as a counterweight to the Jack Kerouac School of Disembodied Poetics, just up the road.

The Doctor himself answered the door. This was important. He had made 108 consecutive deadlines since he started writing for the *San Francisco Examiner* and this improbable streak was on the line. Hunter spoke: "Wantsomecoke, hash, smoke-something? Thanksforcoming." He was surprised, gracious, and a little apologetic. Someone had actually gotten up at three in the morning to deliver beer to him. *Police Story* was on the TV in the background. It lent a pleasant ambient din of sirens, fistfights, and gunfire. Kathy was in the corner, cute and perky, still a total stranger to Mick. Kathy explained Hunter's current process. He was on one of his perpetual speaking tours and he would use his "lectures" as material for the column. He would bait the audience and direct the ensuing give-and-take to his needs, all the while taping. Afterward, he'd retire to his room and work from the recording.

On the whole, this approach worked pretty well. But on that particular evening he had run out of tape during a spirited exchange with four Boulder women. The topic was the social implications of pornography. It had the potential to be a great column, and Hunter was hoping that Mick and Kathy could recreate that portion of the evening. Mick was dubious, not having attended the event. Kathy was optimistic. The two retreated to a corner and left Hunter to Hunter. Recreating isn't easy work. All Mick knew about porn were some case studies saying that you can't use zoning to keep it out of your neighborhood. Nothing firsthand. He decided, instead, to try to get Kathy to apply to law school. Mick knew people in admissions; Hunter hated lawyers.

There was a knock on the door. Hunter turned, "SorryMick-Ididn'tknowifyou'dmakeitsoIorderedsomebackup." Like something that crept out of Hunter's subconscious, a short, sweating, wild-haired, twentysomething kid entered the room holding a baggie aloft. "I got them; I got the 'shrooms," he announced proudly. Now Mick couldn't tell psychedelic mushrooms from grass clippings, but he had an idea that he knew what was in the bag.

It took the untidy youth a good half-hour to make Doc understand that he didn't want to be paid for the drugs. He wanted to be able to say that he'd done mushrooms with Hunter S. Thompson. (Someone was on something already.) He would not accept money from his hero. Hunter wanted the kid to leave, go back to wherever, so he could try to get back to work. What the kid wanted was for Hunter to sign his chest, his greasy, sweaty chest. That seemed reasonable. Someone produced a red Magic Marker. "Hunter Thompson is weird" is what the kid wanted Hunter to write. Hunter proceeded, in capital letters. As he wrote, the sweat dissolved the marker, creating a Steadmanesque drool. Hunter got to the word *weird* and paused. He had forgotten how to spell it. He asked for input. How was it possible that Hunter Thompson couldn't spell *weird*? The combined talent in the room spelled it out for him one letter at a time. The kid left, inscription dripping.

"He'sgonnagetusbusted. He'llgetstoppedbythecopsandpulluphisshirtandsayI'vebeendoing'shroomswithHunterThompson."

Hunter's diction was murky as usual, but the image was crystalline. The kid opening his shirt for the cops, swelling with pride.

Mick hadn't actually witnessed Doc consume so much as a single beer since he had arrived, but the baggie full of mushrooms bore a close resemblance to an evidence bag in his mind. Cops don't much like Hunter. Mick had a future. Time to go.

Hunter didn't make his deadline that night, or any other. Apparently that evening marked the beginning of the end of Hunter and the *Examiner*.

It should be noted that Kathy wasn't really Hunter's wife. All for the best. Hunter's halfhearted attempt to stab her with a ballpoint pen on the flight back to Aspen probably wouldn't have done the marriage any good.

Years later Mick was having lunch with a high powered Denver law firm. A tableful of sharply dressed attorneys were there to evaluate him as a potential associate. Almost the entire lunch was spent discussing his most important qualification: Did he really know Hunter Thompson?

Back in Aspen, one year a district attorney actually got a search warrant for Owl Farm. Along with a lot of nothing, the cops seized a videotape labeled "Child Pornography." The tape turned out to be a PBS panel discussion on the subject. Probably touching the same points as Hunter and the four Boulder women.

When Mick returned to Aspen and became county commissioner, he once again began to receive 3:00 A.M. phone calls from Hunter. Mick was a political ally despite his offensive lifestyle. Politics far outweighed his bad habits.

And so, Mick writes: "Hunter and Nixon and the Evil Developers he hated so well are gone now and so, as a mutual friend put it, I know when the phone rings at 3 A.M., it's probably bad news, in plain English."

The Mayor's Daughter and an Awkward Moment

The "Derby" parties and the Super Bowl parties were late-afternoon events. Family time. If it's family time at your house, then it's family time at Owl Farm. People would feel free to bring their children. Hunter had no problem with children, as long as they were willing to gamble along with everyone else. Given Doc's nocturnal lifestyle, there usually wasn't much chance of running into a child in the kitchen, so it wasn't really any hardship to have them around on these special occasions. It encouraged our best behavior. Besides, I think Hunter probably viewed it as an opportunity to fleece the parents twice.

The gambling at the Kentucky Derby and Super Bowl parties was different from the usual football and basketball wagering.

During the regular seasons there'd be the standard house bet on the game, twenty dollars (a figure that Hunter would always be glad to adjust . . . up), possibly an "over and under" bet, and lots of proposition bets during the course of the game. The quality of thought that went into the wagering varied greatly. Nobody was better informed than Hunter. He poured over the sports pages, the ever-changing betting lines, the injury situations, the matchups—and he wouldn't hesitate to call friends across the country to get inside information to give him an edge.

On the other side, former alpine skiing coach and sports commentator Bob Beattie, filmmaker Bob Rafelson, and Sheriff Braudis could always be counted on to make intelligent, well-informed wagers. There were many others who could be best described as middling ignorant. Then there were the Ewing brothers, Wayne and Andrew. Wayne is a filmmaker who, even when based in L.A., maintained a place in the Roaring Fork Valley. His brother, Andrew, would visit several times a year. Wayne and Andrew were deeply entrenched in Hunter's inner circle. As a rule they were both smart, savvy gamblers; they did their homework. But they had a tendency to get caught up in the moment. Wayne and Andrew would enter the kitchen and immediately start tough negotiations with Hunter over points on the game bet. This could sometimes be a long, painful process. Hunter liked the edge; these guys liked the edge. Then came the over/under: same thing. When this was settled we'd all assume our positions to watch the game.

Sometimes the first proposition bet could come with the opening kickoff. Sometimes it took a while to work into it. Either way, it was a pretty sure thing that one of the Ewing boys would be involved. In the beginning the propositions would be reasonable. A first down this series, whether the next play would be a pass or a run, something that could go either way. Hunter would almost always take up the challenge, and then some of the rest of us would jump in. As the game proceeded, these wagers would slowly increase in recklessness: long-shot first-down attempts, low-percentage chances of scoring on this drive. After a while, the drink flowing, everything else flowing, raucous goodwill abounding, these wagers would move from reckless to irrational: a team scoring late in the game from deep in their own red zone, long, long, field goal attempts.

It was at these times that the intelligent, well-prepared Ewing brothers became the "lemming brothers." This was Hunter's time. He would glow. Hunter thought it morally deficient not to take advantage of someone who was succumbing to his own stupidity. The proposition bets were usually of the five- or ten-dollar variety. The point wasn't just to take all of anyone's money; it wasn't nearly that honorable. The point was to thoroughly embarrass and deeply disgrace the other guy. That was worth the wager. And that was usually the way things turned out. But, as noted, that was during the regular sports seasons. Then there was the Derby, something altogether different.

There was plenty of side betting at the Kentucky Derby parties, but a lot of that kind of energy, out of deference to the non-regulars, was focused on "the pool." For the Derby, the pool involved drawing horses' names out of a hat, a matter of pure luck. Hunter would set it up so that the winner walked away with several hundred dollars. But in light of all the kiddies, the buy-in was never too expensive. If Mommy wanted to buy in for you, great. If a child used his own money, earned shoveling snow over the course of a long, cold winter, that was okay, too. We always respected a young person's right to be fleeced as much as an adult's.

The living room was used mainly by the women to get away from us, and for large overflow events.

The crowd at the Derby parties consisted of the inner circle and their significant others, old friends with their families, and occasional newcomers and guests. Many of the kids who attended these parties had been regulars from an early age and were very hip. They knew the score and were often put in charge of the pools. One good lad, Matthew Goldstein, not only ran the Super Bowl pool but also won it with annoying regularity. Aspen mayor John Bennett, his wife, Janie, and their young daughter, Eleanor, came under the "old friend" category, often attending the special events but not part of the less-savory regular gang.

As the Kentucky Derby itself lasted only minutes, the party would begin a couple of hours before hand. There was always good food and more than enough to drink, of course. Hunter's bedroom TV would be brought into the living room for these occasions, as the assembled crowd was far too big for the kitchen. There was plenty of eating and drinking before the race, a little side betting, and of course the pool. As post time approached, the party would be in full swing. Everybody had a horse, especially the kids.

On one particular Derby day, the mayor's daughter, Eleanor, had coughed up the cash and drawn her horse; she was pretty excited about this new grown-up thing, gambling. Unfortunately, she had a previous engagement that coincided with the exact time of the race itself. It was a strange time to leave, just before the big event, but Eleanor's mom, Janie, a force in her own right, took her daughter in hand, made their excuses with the promise that they would return shortly, and off they went. The race in all its glory came and went in less time than it is possible to have any other kind of meaningful experience. As fate would have it, young Eleanor won the pool without being present. Hunter, after surely wrestling with the prospects of ripping her off, decided that we shouldn't tell Eleanor about her winning but should instead replay the tape of the race and let her experience it as if she were watching it live.

All major sporting events were taped at Owl Farm. An extremely prudent policy, considering the state of consciousness people were capable of achieving by the end of any given competition. It gave a reassuring credibility to the reckoning. Eleanor Bennett and her mother returned to the party after a while. Hunter grabbed a crony and told him to put in the tape of the race. In the meantime he began to set up Eleanor for the big event, building the suspense with all his considerable skills.

Having worked the mayor's daughter into a fever of anticipation, Hunter hit the remote. The room fell silent. Silent, except for the peak volume sounds of the hard-core porno film that appeared on the enormous TV screen. There's something about the audio track of a top-drawer porno film that, when played at high volume, is even more obscene than the visuals. Of course the visuals were pretty good, too. Wrong tape. An easy mistake. There certainly were plenty of tapes lying around in front of the TV. God knows what else was in there. Pandemonium ensued.

With the strangled cry of the wounded and feral, Hunter snatched up the remote, wildly thumbing every button, with zero effect. As later investigations revealed, someone had put a glass down in front of the electric eye that received the signals from the remote. But for now there was only chaos. Hunter flung the remote across the room. Close to a dozen remote controls were in front of him, scattered to either side and on top of his typewriter. He snatched them up one at a time, crazily hitting buttons at random. Small appliances sprang to life—radio, CD player, air-conditioner—each one mocking him in turn, as the porn film played on, still at top volume. Some fled the scene in terror or hysterical laughter. Some discovered a renewed interest in television. All the while, the mayor's sweet young daughter stood impassively, watching closely, waiting for the race to begin.

Courtesy of Nicki Rapp

Hunter expresses his frustration with the remotes as the mayor's daughter watches.

Cleverly's Short Road Trip

Nothing has to be simple. Things can be as complicated, exciting, or horrifying as you want to make them. If you're the kind of person who can say, "Excitement is my copilot," even the most mundane event can become an adventure. If you're the unfortunate fool who happens to, temporarily, find himself in that first person's copilot's seat, you might end up asking yourself, "Why me? Why isn't Excitement here doing his job?"

As usual, it started out simply enough. What could possibly go wrong? The Jeep had to be serviced. Hunter and I would drive six miles to the airport, pick up a rental, and drive both cars back to Owl Farm. When all was done, Hunter would have an extra vehicle, and he and Deborah could take the Jeep in to the garage at their convenience. Cake.

I was asked to come by around three, which I did. When I got there, Hunter was still struggling toward consciousness. I was given to understand there had been nightmares. I wonder what constituted a nightmare in Hunter's mind. I suspect that what the rest of us would consider a terrible nightmare would be another boring night at the office for Doc. Did I really want to know what Hunter's dreams were? No.

I asked Deborah if maybe I should come back later. She said this had to get done now. The rental car place closed after the last flight; it was off-season and the last flight came early. She popped me a beer, and I waited while she continued to try to rouse Hunter.

It had to be Hunter and me on this project because the Jeep rental was also a test drive. Hunter had just received one of his big advances and was thinking about getting a new rig and giving the old one to Deborah. The old Jeep only had thirty thousand miles on it. Practically a new car. This was all a secret, so Deborah didn't know.

I sipped my beer for a while, and eventually Hunter came tottering out of the bedroom. In his bathrobe, kind of shaky. Not exactly ready to go. Three in the afternoon was a little early for Doc on a non-football afternoon. It wasn't Sunday. It wasn't even football season. He said good morning, slipped behind me to his stool, and Deborah began to prepare breakfast. She cut up some fresh fruit, started some eggs and toast. A Bloody Mary sounded good to Hunter, so did a beer and of course a nice big tumbler of Chivas and water. He jammed a cigarette into the holder, lit it, opened "the drawer," and hauled out the coke grinder. "No thanks, Doc. A little early for me. When we get back." Self-control. That's my motto. Then came the hash pipe. Deborah served up the eggs and toast. "None for me, thanks." That meal had come seven or eight hours earlier. Hunter started picking at the food. Sipping the drinks. Breakfast seemed to be coming along nicely.

Two hours later. I'm on my third beer. I've been nursing them, refusing drugs. I have to drive. Hunter has to drive, too, but he has a different set of standards. Deborah, a woman of infinite patience, is a touch agitated. We've called out to the rental car place two, maybe three times. Each time Hunter says that we're on our way, and then asks some question or other—the color of the car, model, accessories—something to suggest to the rental guys that research is being done. As opposed to our sitting around the kitchen getting loaded. Research is not being done. The other thing is being done. At least by someone.

The place will be closed in an hour; they'll go home. It's time to get Hunter dressed. Deborah nags him off his stool and into the bedroom. Fifteen minutes later, Hunter comes out dressed. The afternoon has slipped by. We've gone from having plenty of time to having no time. Let's go. We can't just go, we have to "get ready." Get ready! JESUS FUCKING CHRIST, I think, leaving these incredibly appropriate words unspoken. "Getting ready" means packing up, and I don't mean jammies and a toothbrush. First a new, huge tumbler of scotch. Then a fresh beer; no need to open it, there's an opener in the Jeep. A fresh pack of cigarettes; forget the fact that there are always several packs in the Jeep. A couple of cigarette holders; don't want to run out. The coke grinder. Drag that out, fill it up, and grind, grind, grind. Stick that in a pocket. Finally the hash pipe. Fill that up, stick it in another pocket. Okay, lets go. Six miles to the airport, you never know.

Out to the car. "Do you want me to drive? I'm good, just a couple beers." A naïve question. Hunter always drove, no matter what. As far as I was concerned, this was definitely a "no matter what" situation. We loaded up. I got into the copilot's seat—remember what I said about being the fool in the copilot's seat? Off we went.

We were okay. We had time, a few miles down Highway 82. Cake. So why the hell was he driving so fast? We had time! Why was he weaving through this traffic? We won't have time if we have to go to jail first! Why was he driving like this? Either the answer was painfully obvious or there was no answer at all. I buckled my seatbelt. I never buckle my seatbelt. That's for people who want to survive the crash. I dug my fingers into the sides of the seat, jaw clenched, I felt fillings disintegrating.

There it was, the traffic light, the turn to the airport. Hunter maneuvered into the right-hand turn lane. Okay, he set up the four-wheel drift, tires screaming. We'd done a 180, we were heading up the access road, we took the left toward the terminal, smoke billowing from the tortured tires. We came to a screeching halt in front of the terminal, a perfect parallel-parking job. Unfortunately, it wasn't a parallel-parking situation. It was a straight-in parking situation. I knew this because, (1) that's the way it had been for all the decades and decades that we'd both lived here, and (2) that was the way ALL THE OTHER CARS WERE PARKED. Hunter was lighting the hash pipe. As the smoke from our exhaust and burning tires was clearing outside, the other smoke was beginning to permeate the interior. I looked around nervously. Shit, two uniforms approaching from the rear, their brisk gait suggesting that they're on duty. Shit. One airport security, one sheriff's deputy.

I powered down my window. Hunter's stayed up. Thank God, they were coming to my side. Instead of sticking their noses in the window to look for probable cause, they stopped about ten feet away. Airport security. "Hi, do you think you could park . . ." The guard made a series of hand gestures, kind of sketching out how he'd like us to rethink things. "Hi, officer," I responded. "Sure, sure, ha ha! We were just about to do that. Ha ha! Thanks." Hunter, wearing a cheerfully accommodating smile, hash pipe replaced by his cigarette holder, slowly slipped the Jeep into gear and carefully backed up and reparked. Perfect citizen, perfect driver, perfect parking job. The officers were standing there watching. We got out, nodding, nervous smiles, making a little wave of appreciation for the responsible officers doing their responsible jobs responsibly.

We entered the terminal. It was almost deserted. The last flight had arrived, the last bag had been claimed. The concessions were in the process of shutting down. All except for one. There was a small crowd around one of the rental car booths. Our rental car booth. Could it be that we were expected? Maybe all those phone calls saying, "Here we come?" Of course. Hunter Thompson was coming to pick up a car. There were plenty of people who thought that might be fun to watch.

We neared the booth, and I hung back. His rental, his fans, he could handle this. And he did, smiling, nodding, and chatting amiably. The rental car guys were grinning and nodding back. There was only the one problem, the usual problem: they could hardly understand a word he was saying. I could see he was getting frustrated. They seemed friendly enough, but they weren't responding. I looked out the large plate-glass window behind the counter. The cops seemed to have stationed themselves out there on the sidewalk and were pointing and talking. If things started to go south, they could go south fast, really fast. I was beginning to get a little edgy.

I wandered up behind Hunter. I smiled at a counter guy. "Do you think you could just give us the paperwork." The counter guy grinned back. I could see him thinking, English, one of them speaks English. He was clearly relieved. He slid the papers to Hunter, who was happy that these people finally understood him. The tension that briefly raced through the crowd dissipated. Hunter breezed through the forms and returned them with a credit card. It was almost over. The counter guy reached for some keys and gave us a concerned look. "Which one of you is driving?"

I lean over the counter. "Which one of us do you want to drive?"

He was a little sheepish. "You?"

"That's fine." I snatched the keys. Hunter gave me a knowing look. Anything to keep these fools happy. We left the building. Hunter lunged for the keys. "Hey Doc, let me take it. You'll have it all week."

Hunter, the picture of generosity, acquiesced. "Sure you go ahead."

What I was thinking was, "Jesus Christ Almighty, if I get stopped driving Hunter's car, with all the stuff in there, I won't see the light of day or breathe free air for twenty years." I headed for a bright red Jeep Cherokee in the rental lot.

We caravanned back to Woody Creek, remarkably without incident. Hunter, clearly first in his driver's ed. class, now doing postgraduate work. Advanced degrees upcoming. We passed the Woody Creek Tavern, ten miles per hour, bright red Jeep, dark green Jeep, both of us waving as if from floats in a parade. We pulled into Owl Farm. "It's great Doc, you'll love it," I exclaimed, gesturing at the shiny new Jeep. "Aren't you coming in?" Hunter asked. "No, no, it's been a long day, a little tired, gotta feed the cats," I responded. "I'll see you down the road. . . . I'll drive."

The Sheriff Reflects on the Neighbor

The term *neighbor* ran deep in Hunter's veins. A good neighbor, in Woody Creek, posed no threat, might help out around the farm, and would, in some situations, be invited to the kitchen. Many kitchen regulars were Creekers, but not all Creekers were welcome in the kitchen. The "hood" was fairly stable, not in the psychological sense by any means, but in terms of residency. The low-density zoning and the premium cost of living, even in a mobile home near the Tavern, resulted in low turnover.

The valley still had the fading memory of its agricultural roots, and a few ranches and farms were still working. Some of them were of the "gentleman" genre, but the creeping castle-ization of trophy homes, a malignancy abounding in and around Aspen, was also invading Woody Creek.

Hunter had condemned the flow of "excrement" from the "Merchant Fortress" of Aspen in the "Woody Creek Manifesto," a one-pager that made its debut at the home of Ed Bastian (HST's next-door neighbor) during a summer picnic. The paper was read aloud to a group of twenty by Don Johnson of *Miami Vice* fame, a neighbor and a regular at Owl Farm. Don often read from Hunter's work in the kitchen and was damn good. On this day he poured his heart into the Manifesto, which condemned the sprawl from Aspen that was entering Woody Creek. He stumbled on *trigonometric*, though, having had neither to memorize nor to deliver many polysyllabic words in his acting career.

Ed Bastian with Bob and Hunter on Ed's porch, where more than one manifesto first saw the light of day.

The poster child of the imminent sea change in the neighborhood was Floyd Watkins. This corpulent transplant from Miami bought a beautifully rustic spread spanning about a mile of

Woody Creek and transformed it into what looked like a gated Kentucky bluegrass horse farm, without the horses. White fences replaced the split rails, the ancient ranch house was supplanted by a stone chateau; Woody Creek itself was contoured by bulldozers into ten or twelve linked cascades and two manmade ponds, which were stocked with non-native trophy trout.

Hunter tried to accept Watkins and the specter surrounding him, but Floyd just didn't fit in. We speculated occasionally about whether he had made his fortune breaking legs for shylocks in Florida. This would not normally be a fatal flaw for Hunter. In fact, under different circumstances, Floyd's history might have added to his cachet with HST. But his total disregard for the environment laid a stigma on him that was only to spread and fester in his relationship with Hunter. Floyd wanted acceptance but just didn't know how to make it happen. Change after change to his land led him to acquire bête noir status with the Doc. And the Doc loved having a target in his crosshairs.

My office got the call. Floyd's trout had been found floating belly up in his two ponds one morning, and he insisted that they had been poisoned by Hunter, following a string of ugly verbal encounters and threats.

I loathed investigations of Hunter. His activities were rarely criminal, and when they were, they were usually borderline misdemeanor in quality. But being Hunter's friend and being Hunter's sheriff was a balancing high-wire act. If Floyd was to be believed, these trout were worth up to a thousand dollars per copy, and the dead school could be worth a major felony, if indeed a crime were involved. Floyd started his rant with an allegation that the crime would not get a fair investigation because of his persona-non-grata status and my friendship with Hunter.

There might have been a few species that Hunter would poison—skunks under his house or foxes that were threats to his domestic peafowl—but he preferred to shoot four-legged pests, so the poisoning of trout was way outside his M.O., even for revenge. He respected most life.

As my staff started the trout poisoning investigation, they learned that the Colorado Division of Wildlife laboratory was not equipped to do a "needle in the haystack" search for any toxin that would have caused this massive death toll of the "golden" or other precious trout. We identified a private lab that might assist us and sent several specimens of fish tissue and pond water to their scientists. Floyd told me that he was going to amp up his homeland security by bunking with his son, Lance, in the back of a Chevy Suburban just inside the driveway leading to his property. Of course they would be heavily armed. They would be the night watch.

I had already linked certain occurrences of alleged aberrant behavior on Hunter's part with the arrival of new female candidates for the "live-in/sleep-in" editorial assistant job slot. Like a lad in junior high, Hunter would try to impress these beauties with childish pranks that lived up to many of the crazy acts he had written about, whether true or not. This was the gonzo way.

The day of the report on the "trouticide," my wife, Ivy, and I were dining at the Woody Creek Tavern. Hunter walked in with a young blonde, and the two joined our table for drinks and chatter. They had arrived in Hunter's red convertible, top down, and Hunter was frisky and animated. When I informed him of Watkins's enhanced security measures, Hunter listened with interest. He declared his innocence vis-à-vis the poisoning, but being accused piqued his revenge reflex and I could see the wheels grinding. "I think this situation calls for some full automatic," he said to the three of us, while sipping on a tall Chivas and water. I shrugged, with a smile. Ivy and I went home, and Hunter and the assistant candidate lingered on.

I was paged before sunrise—never a good thing. This one sounded bad. Floyd had called 911 at "zero dark 30"— cop-speak for the wee hours before dawn—to report machine gun fire at the end of the driveway where he and his son were sleeping in the big SUV. Floyd reported that he had opened the electric gate to his drive with the remote control and seen taillights receding downhill from his location. A chase commenced. Floyd was gaining on the lights when he saw the vehicle ahead turn to the right in a four-wheel drift into the driveway of George Stranahan, another prominent Woody Creeker. Floyd followed the unidentified vehicle into the drive, which dead-ended at George's house. Later, George stated that at 4:00 A.M. he was awakened by a commotion outside. He said that he looked out the window and saw Hunter and a blonde in a red convertible being screamed at by Floyd and his son. He said that both sides were armed in some fashion. George's wife, Patti, joined him at the window, assessed the situation, and went outside. She intervened, and things cooled down. Both teams left the field. Hunter went to Owl Farm, and Floyd went to his telephone.

I had always advised my staff to treat any suspects, including my close friends, with the objectivity, fairness, and suspicion that our policies dictated. I checked in with the night shift and found out that the deputy who had responded to the Watkins residence had taken statements from Floyd and his son. He then walked the road near its intersection with Floyd's driveway and found a fairly large pile of "brass," expended cartridges, of the nine-millimeter variety. He gathered the evidence and tagged it. The case was open and active.

Hunter called much later in the day and asked if anything was going on, just an innocent, general inquiry. "Of course there's something going on, Doc!" I gave him an abbreviated version of the Miranda warning and advised him to lawyer up, advice that I would give to anyone in the suspect category.

Meanwhile, reports from the forensic fish lab came back. The poor finned bastards had died of a copper OD; the tissue samples revealed a copper content a bazillion times the lethal level. Nobody at Watkins's Beaver Run Ranch was talking. "We don't know anything about copper, and these trout were healthy for months" was their line. But an informant who insisted on remaining anonymous (and eligible for a piece of the reward put up by Floyd) said that he'd seen Floyd's kid, Lance, and Roberto, the ranch manager, out in a rowboat on one of the ponds the day before the massacre pouring liquid out of a five-gallon can into the pond. Follow-up investigation yielded the discovery of empty cans of Cupertine, an algaecide with an active ingredient called copper. Case closed. Case number one, anyway.

Floyd wasn't nearly as talkative anymore. But Hunter, temporarily out of the spotlight, reveled in Floyd's chagrin. In addition to falsely accusing him of killing the trout, Floyd had proven that his failure to meet all the criteria for simple decency should be combined with his misstatements and he should be driven from Woody Creek Valley entirely.

My detectives called the Denver office of the United States BATF—Bureau of Alcohol, Tobacco, and Firearms. Our questions centered upon whether HST had filed any paperwork indicative of possession of fully automatic weaponry. "Two," the agent said. Innocently, he had released confidential IRS info, and he called back shortly to retract his statement. The investigators came to me for some direction. I called ATF and asked that an agent come to Aspen in person.

Meanwhile, Hunter's lawyer was trying to control his client. "Floyd's credibility should be scrutinized and he should be neutered and impeached as a witness," Hunter complained. "He knew that his child moron killed those fish and he caused precious public funds to be wasted in investigative costs. I say we bill that pig-faced cocksucker!" In a small town with two daily newspapers and Thompson-worshipping journalists, Hunter was grooving on this Kabuki theater.

Two young ATF agents arrived from Denver the next day. The facts, which they had provided the day before, illegally, were central to any affidavit in the quest for a warrant to search Owl Farm for a machine gun. I couldn't believe it when they said that they would perjure themselves before copping to the mistake. They went so far as to suggest that, in the right hands, semiautomatic pistol fire could be as fast as a submachine gun. I was still loathing the case, but learning more about my friend Hunter's chronic paranoia.

The deputy DA in Aspen, Mac Myers, was our legal advisor. The firing of any weapons near or at an occupied residence constituted felony menacing and/or endangerment. The circumstantial evidence was borderline, but Mac was already in a dialogue with HST's lawyer. Hunter was publicly posing the possibility that he had been attacked by a "giant killer porcupine, a beast without a back," while driving in his open car. The press ate it up. They were apoplectic with joy: GONZO JOURNALIST ATTACKED BY GIANT PORCUPINE, screamed the headlines.

Hunter asked me for a man-to-man, men of the world, off-the-record meeting. I consented. At the Tavern, he bitched about Floyd, the ATF, me, the DA and his lawyer. It was his nature to deny culpability in any and all events when negative eventualities knocked on his door. He deflected all blame and was a firm believer in conspiracy theories. He knew that I knew that he owned a machine gun. He knew that, if asked under oath, I would attest to the existence of that type of weapon at the farm. He knew that he had miscalculated badly; he knew it the very instant that the Suburban came roaring out of Beaver Run Ranch. He knew that he was pissed off and he knew that the elected DA, Milt Blakey, hated his guts.

"Couldn't you do better than a killer porcupine?" I asked. The man was a creative genius. A killer porcupine? He deflected the question. "Bob, why did you grin like a Cheshire cat that night when I said Floyd needed a dose of full auto?"—suggesting that, by grinning, I was an accomplice. I didn't think I had.

In the end, Thompson's lawyer and the deputy DA crafted the deal. If HST delivered and surrendered a machine gun to the district attorney's office, no charges would be pursued.

The following day Hunter walked into Mac's office with a heavy garbage bag. In the bag was a Schmeuser nine-millimeter World War II–vintage machine gun hacksawed in half and smeared with naval gel, a rust remover. "A perfectly good weapon had to die to resolve this bullshit case. You pigs have prevailed, this time."

Floyd accused all of us of a cover-up, but made no further comments about gunfire or the trout kill.

I told Hunter that any further investigations of his misdeeds would be referred to outside agencies. He nodded in acceptance of my decision. I was disturbed but felt clean. The next case lay waiting. Grinned like a Cheshire cat? I don't think so.

The legend of a rampaging killer porcupine endures in Woody Creek. Sometimes on moonless nights, one can almost feel its presence.

Cleverly Explains How Hunter "Goes Off" Occasionally

Hunter's short fuse was a thing of legend. No one liked it, but those of us who were around him all the time took it for granted and did our best to overlook it. Most of us could just leave if it got to be too much, and people who lived at the farm had their hiding places. The thing was, it never lasted long. It was kind of amazing to see someone go from normal to a rage and then back to normal again in such a short span of time. That's why it wasn't so bad; you knew he'd be back.

Unfortunately, people who weren't in the know could become the object of his wrath. They took it a little harder. (If you want a good example of this, watch Wayne Ewing's *Breakfast with Hunter* and enjoy, or watch in horror, as the Doctor takes off on a movie director who was auditioning to work on the film *Fear and Loathing in Las Vegas*.)

Hunter was basically a decent, good-hearted human being. He didn't have to worry about his buddies, but once in a while, after he'd taken off on a stranger, he'd feel terrible afterward, especially when the individual didn't deserve it, which was usually the case. That was what happened in the case of the stuttering professor.

Hunter's two "letters" books, *The Proud Highway* and *Fear and Loathing in America*, were the last books that he did any substantial publicity for. When *The Proud Highway* was published in 1997 a publication party was held in New York, complete with Doc's celebrity friends, old and new, and the usual phalanx of nubiles and VIPs. There were also TV appearances, the whole deal.

One sunny afternoon that summer, Hunter and I were sitting in his kitchen. He was back in Woody Creek on a break from these publicity efforts. The peacocks were wandering around the grounds, squawking at the occasional passing car or furtive chipmunk. There was a random assortment of firearms lying around the kitchen, just in case anyone had a sudden impulse to run outside and blast the crap out of something. The women weren't anywhere to be seen, perhaps in town on errands.

Owl Farm and Woody Creek were beautiful that time of year. All greens and yellows, foliage and sunshine. On any given day at that hour the blinds in Hunter's kitchen could be closed or open, depending on whether it was the end of one day or the beginning of the next. The blinds were open that day, letting the sun stream in on us. The television was on, as it was 24-7. This particular afternoon, the sound was off, but the TV itself had to be on in case current events conspired to interfere with our meditations. One has to stay current at all costs.

We were both in fine humor, discussing matters of importance, when the phone rang. Hunter's phone was always on "speaker" so that all present could eavesdrop. The caller was a teacher from a major university. This guy either taught a course on Hunter, or taught a course of which Hunter was a major part; I don't remember which. Apparently the prof had booked a speaking engagement for Doc at a large venue in his university town and he wanted to discuss some details. Clearly he held Hunter in some sort of awe. Just as clearly, they'd never met. Not that Hunter didn't merit the awe; it's just that those who knew Doc knew that an attitude of awe rarely paid off.

After a bit of discussion, Hunter allowed that he had a few questions for the professor. Now, this guy had booked Hunter into exactly one gig, while Hunter had been booked into countless engagements in his career, which gave him a huge edge. Hunter's mind worked faster than most people's, including your average academic. He could be an impatient man. He never suffered fools gladly—at times he didn't suffer anyone gladly. This was evolving into one of those times. Hunter was peppering the prof with questions, demanding details that weren't immediately available. As the grilling continued, it was clear that this guy was becoming increasingly upset with himself for disappointing the great man. Hunter in turn was becoming more agitated. I guess it was inevitable: Hunter went off.

A cloud passed over the sun in Woody Creek, the peacocks fell silent, and a chilling breeze came through the window. Now, I knew this pyrotechnic display was a state of mind that would pass—and a fine, affable gentleman would soon enough be restored to us. But for those who didn't know Hunter, there was no reason to think that his rage—so towering and so deep—would not last forever. In this particular case, Hunter's rant was phrased in the form of a question, so he stopped and waited for a reply. We waited, and we waited. There was only silence from the despairing professor. Finally, Hunter loosed another barrage of invective at peak volume, hoping, you know, to jump-start the conversation. More pregnant moments passed, and then out of the speaker came what sounded like a random assortment of vowels and consonants, maybe some syllables.

Jesus, the guy was a stutterer or, more correctly, a recovering stutterer—he'd been fine early in the conversation, but now that the pressure was on, he'd fallen apart completely. I couldn't stand it. Hunter had broken him; he'd taken a perfectly nice man who clearly idolized him and reduced him to what I'm sure the man hated most about himself. I looked at Hunter; his face was contorted with shock and remorse.

I empathized with the poor professor, his was a tragic case. But it was the grief on Hunter's face that got me. I don't know if I'd ever seen anything just like it before. I charged out of the kitchen and into the living room—just in case I couldn't suppress my laughter.

It took me lots of time and substances to regain my composure. When I returned to the kitchen I found Hunter still on the phone, coping with the awkwardness of the situation as best he could—in his own particular fashion.

I guess you could say that the art of apology wasn't something that Hunter ever really bothered to master. I'm sure if he had, he would have been great at it, but it wasn't his thing. He was, however, talking soothingly at the speakerphone. I paused for a moment, hoping to hear a non-stuttered reply, but there was only silence from the other end of the line. Hunter kept on.

I felt awfully bad for the guy, but I'm sure Hunter felt worse. I could see that right away. Of course that didn't mean that he wouldn't do it again as soon as the mood struck him.

As I walked toward my truck, the cloud had passed and the sun was shining brightly, the breeze had warmed and the peacocks were again strutting and squawking. I felt these men should be left alone to their business.

DOCUDRAMA

I was trotting across the lawn toward the driveway waving two pornographic calendars; the young filmmakers were trotting faster. This was kind of surprising because they were burdened by a lot of heavy equipment. Of course they had more incentive, and several more trips to make. The electric cords and fixtures that they were trailing must have made it awkward for them.

Of all the film crews I'd encountered at Owl Farm over the years, these guys seemed the most professional. What I know about filmmaking would fit in a shot glass with plenty of room left over for whiskey. So, when I say they seemed professional, I mean they had lots and lots of equipment. Big bright lights, big shiny cameras.

I'd first encountered them around four in the afternoon that same day. I was heading out the door and they were pulling into the driveway of Owl Farm. When they got out of their rig, I placed myself between them and the door. Hunter's friends tended to screen strangers. They could see what I was doing and good-naturedly said that it was okay, they were expected. Hunter and I had just been having a nice, neighborly afternoon visit, nothing degenerate, so I introduced myself, wished them luck with whatever they were up to, and scrammed.

A few hours later I was making myself some dinner when Hunter's voice came on my answering machine. "Michael, are you there? Pick up. You have to get over here. I need help." This not being my first rodeo, I gauged the actual urgency in his voice as moderate, listened, and ate my dinner. When I finished, I speed-dialed Owl Farm and when Hunter's machine picked up I just said, "It's me. I'm coming right over," and headed out.

I arrived in Hunter's kitchen minutes later. Doc was on his stool, and the two film guys were there. Thirtysomething, clean-cut, and sober, they looked fine to me. Hunter gave me a hug, told me to grab a beer, and hauled out the coke grinder to make me feel welcome. As the guys and I were introducing ourselves I peered around them and into the living room. Lots of high-tech equipment in there.

Filmmakers. These guys were filmmakers. They'd driven out from L.A. just to interview Hunter. They were making a documentary on George McGovern and his presidential bid, which had been the inspiration for Hunter's book *Fear and Loathing on the Campaign Trail*. The senator had called personally and asked if Hunter would do him a favor and talk to these guys. It had been set up for weeks. Sure. Time passes, moods change. Now they were at Owl Farm and things weren't going so well. It had been hours since they'd arrived and all they'd been able to accomplish was to move about half their equipment into the living room and piss Hunter off.

They were nice fellas. Smart, courteous, and professional. What could they have done wrong? Nothing. But timing is everything. Hunter simply didn't feel like being bothered at that particular moment, so he decided that they were half-assed and ill-prepared. And now they were paying an unpleasant price. I was there for what? To back Hunter up? To help boot the poor bastards out? I really didn't feel like helping Doc crucify them, because, to me, they seemed whole-assed and well-prepared. I didn't, however, mind hanging around, swilling a couple of beers, and snorting some after-dinner gag. So, I was in for the show.

Now, this being-interviewed-on-camera thing was something that Hunter had done a thousand times, and when he was enjoying himself, he was great at it. He was smart enough and professional enough that, even in traction, he should have been able to pull it off with no trouble. Hunter felt fine, but was disinclined to put himself out on this particular evening. I tried to reason with him. Just do it, get it over with. They'll leave. It seemed so simple. Too simple, apparently. Hunter raged, I mollified, the filmmakers wrung their hands. Hunter and I drank, the filmmakers wrung their hands. Hunter and I snorted, the filmmakers wrung their hands. Hunter accused them of knowing nothing of his work. Jesus, they had every book he'd ever written with them. Not new copies, either—beat-up, dog-eared pages marked, passages highlighted. They knew a lot more about his work than I ever would. The interview was about as close to scripted as you could get. Piece of cake. No surprises, no ambushes. I suggested that we read from some of the highlighted stuff. I suggested that I read. Okay.

Hunter, a funny writer, enjoyed hearing his work read, liked to hear people laughing at it. Like clouds parting in the middle of a terrible storm, a patch of blue appeared with a couple little birds flying around up there. Hunter lightened. I hoped this would be a window of opportunity. "Okay, go get your stuff," Hunter said. The technical guy charged out of the kitchen. He proceeded to set up these huge lights and what-all in the living room. The interviewer guy stayed with Hunter and me in the kitchen. I kept reading. There was lots of setting-up going on out there; they had tons of shit, and it was taking time. The clouds closed in again; no more blue sky. The birds were gone, probably dead. The window closed; too bad. The abuse resumed. I felt bad for the guys, although, I must confess, making them think that everything was going to be all right was a nice touch.

My mind raced. I was running out of gambits to try to make the situation less ugly. Then I thought of it: the calendar. The calendar combined the two things Hunter loved most: naked women and Hunter. "Doc, have they seen the calendar yet?"

I had produced a dirty calendar a couple of years earlier. Hunter had been asked to write a one-line endorsement to try to help sell the thing and he ended up writing a whole essay. It had its own page. The calendar was coveted by the hip, in-crowd, from New York to L.A. It was a fine bit of writing, never published anywhere else. And the images were depraved.

No, they hadn't seen the calendar, but Hunter had run out of them. As I had hoped, the thought seemed to cheer him. All those naked girls, his own words. I said I'd go back to my cabin and grab a couple. I should have considered the downside of my leaving. When I returned to the kitchen I saw that things had gone to a place that is usually reached in a handbasket. The guys were huddled by the front door clearly planning a break. Hunter was raging. I heard the door opening, looked into the living room to see them heading out with armloads of equipment. "Jesus, Hunter, at least sign these for them." Hunter was beaming, his mission accomplished. He cheerfully signed the calendars, and I chased after the filmmakers. I caught up with them at their van and pressed the calendars on them. They were grateful and thanked me for trying to help. That was it. I went inside and visited with Hunter while the film guys continued to make trips loading up equipment. I said goodnight, and left before they had finished.

FUCK

The next set of documentarians arrived while Hunter and I were sitting in the kitchen chewing the fat and watching some tube. They were expected—I mean, God help them if they hadn't been—but not by me. It had been several weeks since the last cinematic incident at Owl Farm. Maybe Hunter thought it would be a nice surprise for me to see more movie guys coming through the door, or maybe he didn't think it worth mentioning. All of a sudden they were in the kitchen. Earnest and beaming. Owl Farm! Hunter Thompson's lair! Just like they'd imagined it! Oh, yeah.

There were two guys, Steve Anderson, director of the narrative feature *The Big Empty,* and a sound technician/cameraman. Both were sharp. The last guys were sharp, too, but sharp isn't enough. Dumb luck is what it takes, and these guys were lucky, at least that night. Hunter was in a fine mood and ready for whatever was going to happen next. So this new crew was welcomed, and we introduced ourselves. Once again the subject of the film wasn't Hunter. Why would anyone make a film about something other than Hunter? Remarkably, their subject was interesting anyway. It was the word *fuck*. They had been crisscrossing the country interviewing well-known and influential people about their attitudes re. *fuck*. Clearly, this was a high-concept film. The kind of out-of-the-box, lateral-thinking sort of thing that appealed to Doc. I was appalled.

The guys accepted some beers, and we made small talk, eventually getting around to their project. The list of people they'd spoken to, and were planning on talking to, was impressive. Filmmaker Kevin Smith, conservative film critic Michael Medved, columnist Judith Martin (Miss Manners), rapper Ice-T, singer Alanis Morissette, newsman Sam Donaldson, porn actor Ron

Jeremy, and a bunch of stand-up comedians whose names are more or less household words.

Hunter left the room to shine himself up for the camera. While he was gone we discussed the film: the hypothetical Southern white guy who would brain you for using the word *fuck* around the womenfolk but who uses the word *nigger* around them with impunity, people who think you ought to be allowed to bellow *fuck* in the schoolyard at recess time. These movie dudes were serious guys who wanted to make a serious and funny film. When Hunter returned, both guys had to get to setting up. They gave us a tape to watch, a rough cut of a couple of interviews. We popped it in, and were immediately enthused. The first interview was with Ben (God) Bradlee. It goes without saying that he was lucid, brilliant. We agreed with everything he said, glancing at each other, nodding in agreement with every word he uttered. Freedom-of-speech stuff, nothing unexpected, though. The surprise came with the next interview: Pat "April Love" Boone. As you might expect, he disapproved of this kind of language. What was unexpected was that he was kind of reasonable and articulate. No ranting right-wing prick, he simply talked about good manners and propriety. Hunter and I were impressed. Not enough to take any vows of pure speech, but we had to give old Pat a little credit.

By the time the tape was over, the guys had finished setting up. We congratulated the boys on their work. How the hell did they get Pat Boone to do an interview on this subject? Hunter was still in a good mood; it was getting late, prime time for him, bedtime for me. The movie guys had to go with the flow. I said goodnight; they went to work.

Fuck, directed by Steve Anderson, premiered at the AFI Los Angeles International Film Festival in April 2005. The promotions for the film billed Hunter's segment as "one of his last inter-views."

One Bright Shining Moment: The Forgotten Summer of George McGovern, directed by Stephen Vittoria, premiered in September 2005. The film featured Gore Vidal, Gloria Steinem, Warren Beatty, Dick Gregory, Gary Hart, Frank Mankiewicz, Howard Zinn, Jim Bouton, Sen. Jim Abourezk, Rev. Malcolm Boyd, and Ron Kovic. No Hunter S. Thompson.

In the eighties, Hunter was in great demand on campus. His appearances were contingent upon his receiving, prior to taking the stage, a brown paper bag with thousands of dollars in small bills inside.

I had watched videos of some of these gigs with Hunter at the farm. They generally followed the same format: opening remarks, usually timely and provocative; Q&A, with the As ranging from brief to epic; and then a closing riff.

While viewing the tapes, Hunter, as with everything, analyzed his performance, praising himself or delivering brutally honest self-criticism. I remember one review during which Hunter kept stopping and rewinding and then replaying the tape at the same point. "What are you doing?" I asked. He said, "Watch. You'll see when the whisky overcomes the cocaine." Hunter played the tape and marked to the minute when he started slurring his words.

Before his performances, Hunter, offstage, would snort enough gag to jump-start a diesel engine and then walk out into the lights. There was always a bottle of Chivas and ice and water onstage, and during his performance he'd swill a lot of Scotch. At best, his mumbling was hard for the uninitiated to understand. And during his appearances, when the Scotch caught up with—and then passed—the gag, well, incomprehension was the order of the day. During this VHS viewing, he said, "See? Right there! I can't talk anymore. Even I can't understand myself. I have to remember to schedule a two-minute break to walk offstage, snort up, and get the chemicals in balance. The students deserve that." That was Hunter. Considerate to a fault.

I got a call one evening in 1987. Hunter asked if I would meet with him and a Secret Service agent the next day at the Holiday Inn in Aspen. The agent had requested an interview with Hunter at Owl Farm. Hunter countered by suggesting a meeting in a room he rented at the motel. He wanted no agents, no agencies, at the farm. Lessons had been learned.

Apparently during a show at Marquette University in Wisconsin, Hunter had stated to the audience, "You're mostly Jesuits, and Jesuits understand guilt." He went on to condemn George H. W. Bush, Reagan's vice president, as the most guilty man in Washington. "In fact," Hunter said, "he's so guilty that he should be tarred and feathered, tied to a rail, and dumped outside the Capitol."

It is the mandate of the Secret Service to investigate any real or perceived threats against those who are protected by the agency. This includes the VP. After the Milwaukee office read about Hunter's suggestion to the students at Marquette, the Milwaukee bureau called the Denver office, and agent Larry Hoppe drew the assignment.

Hunter had brushed up against scores of Secret Service men when he was covering Nixon, McGovern, Carter, and others. Having sized him up, they liked him, and Hunter got access to the candidates.

No doubt Larry Hoppe had read Hunter's file, but policy is policy, and formalities are requisite. I left the brilliant Colorado sunshine at 10:00 A.M. and started down the dark corridor to Hunter's room. My eyes had yet to adjust to the gloom, so I sensed rather than saw a male figure approaching me. "Dr. Thompson?" he said.

"No. I'm Bob Braudis, Pitkin County Sheriff."

"Larry Hoppe, U.S. Secret Service. Are you here for my interview with Mr. Thompson?"

"Yes" I said. "Room 162."

I knocked at the door, and it was opened by Deborah Fuller. I introduced Larry to Deborah and we entered to find Hunter rising from the Inn's armchair in his true gentlemanly fashion. "Good morning, Dr. Thompson. Larry Hoppe, United States Secret Service."

"You got ID, Larry?"

Hoppe showed his tin and credentials. He gave Hunter the background leading to this interview/interrogation and explained that he first had to complete a questionnaire of the "suspect."

"Full name, please."

"Hunter S. Thompson"

"S stands for Stockton?"

Smile. "Yes, sir."

Place of birth, date of birth, current address, etc., standard cop fare. Then the agent asked about level of education. Hunter said college, and Larry asked where. "Columbia," Hunter said. My brows rose, but I stood mute. News to me.

"Major," the agent asked.

"Chemotherapy," Hunter replied.

Larry wrote it down. "Do you have a Colorado driver's license?"

"Yes."

"Might it be expired?" posed agent Hoppe.

"Well, let's see," Hunter said as he fumbled for his wallet. Then: "Goddamnit, Deborah! You let my license expire!" Larry had done his homework. He asked about weapons and Hunter gave him a partial list, the legal version of his inventory. The conversation became less formal. I assured Hoppe that Hunter was no threat to Bush or the social fabric. Soon Hoppe opened his briefcase and removed two or three of HST's bestsellers and requested that Hunter sign them. Hunter, of course, obliged proudly and cordially.

I found it ironic that an investigator would end his interview with a request for a favor. But how many times would this opportunity arise?

Hunter and Hoppe kept up a correspondence for years, through Hoppe's retirement. Hunter attracted a full spectrum of fans and recognized quality and sincerity.

Hoppe left the Inn. Hunter, Deborah, and I went to the restaurant. Hunter ordered everything on the menu, nibbled at some, had it all boxed, and went home. I went back to work.

Cleverly Tells of the Lisl Auman Crusade

The only thing necessary for the triumph of evil is for good men to do nothing.

—EDMUND BURKE

The first phone call I remember getting from Hunter went something like this: "Michael, this is Hunter Thompson. I hear there's a conspiracy. If there's a conspiracy, I want in." That happened so long ago I don't really remember what the conspiracy was—or if there really was a conspiracy at all. It might have had something to do with a gag political campaign my friend cartoonist Chris Cassatt was mounting. Perhaps by the time the news reached Hunter's ears it had morphed into something larger and more serious than it actually was. It was cool to get a call from Doc, and it was my first experience with how deep his political passions ran.

Hunter was a crusader, a gonzo Knight Templar; a cause was mother's milk to him. During an election year his hunger was easy to feed. Drive the hated Republicans and right-wingers from office. Success meant elation; failure was darkness. George W. Bush's election to a second term was very, very bad; total darkness. As passionate and as close as he was to national politics, it couldn't match the intimacy of his crusade to save Lisl Auman. Lisl brought politics to the most personal level. Lisl's situation was emblematic of everything Hunter despised about the "system." It was a huge power structure versus one young woman, revenge rather than justice. On the face of it, the simple facts of the case seemed so obvious that any low-grade moron could see the horrible injustice that was being perpetrated. It was difficult to understand how it could have happened; it was a fight worthy of Hunter S. Thompson. Hunter was up against every cop and prosecutor in Denver. He had them outnumbered.

In the early seventies, a judge lay in bed in Aspen Valley Hospital. He was in crummy shape. Most of his medical problems were self-inflicted and serious. It was the booze. Someone had brought him a copy of *Fear and Loathing in Las Vegas,* by Hunter S. Thompson, an author he wasn't particularly familiar with. The judge recovered, kicked the booze, and returned to the bench. He said that he laughed himself well. He gave Hunter credit for saving his life.

Decades later, a young girl in the Denver County Jail was given a copy of the same book. By the time she wrote to Hunter in January 2001, she was in the Colorado Women's Correctional Facility in Canon City, serving a sentence of life without possibility of parole. She was told that Hunter's books were banned from the Colorado Department of Corrections libraries. If that was true, she had read her last book by HST. The girl, Lisl Auman, wrote:

Mr. Hunter S. Thompson:

 I laughed out loud while reading "Fear and Loathing in Las Vegas," during my stay (13 months) at the Denver County Jail. Thank you for helping to bring a smile to my face.

 I am now a hostage . . .

Hunter was moved by the letter and responded. It was the beginning of an odyssey that he and Lisl shared until the day Hunter died.

Lisl Auman had been convicted of felony murder. The murder in question had been committed by someone else while Lisl was handcuffed and locked in the backseat of a Denver police cruiser. Those were facts that nobody disputed.

I first heard about Lisl's letter a few nights after Hunter wrote her back. I was over at Owl Farm for a few pops, and Doc had me read aloud both Lisl's letter and his response. I remembered seeing TV coverage of the incident at the time, but not the sad details.

Denver police officer Bruce VanderJagt had been gunned down. He was a handsome guy with a beautiful young family. Forty-seven years old, an ex-Marine, he had his master's degree and was working on a Ph.D. The city of Denver was, rightfully, outraged at his murder, and the Denver law enforcement community was so pissed off they couldn't see straight. The shooter was an asshole skinhead named Matthaus Jachnig. After killing VanderJagt, the kid turned the gun on himself. The cops still demanded their pound of flesh, and with the actual murderer dead, Lisl Auman was the only available donor.

It happened in November 1997. Lisl Auman was twenty-one years old. She was trying to escape an ugly living situation in Buffalo Creek, a small mountain town outside Denver. Lisl needed help getting her stuff out of a rooming house that was also home to her jerk boyfriend. The registration on her car had expired, so she needed transportation. Her dad offered to help, but not until the weekend; he had to work. She sought out her old friend Deme. Deme's skinhead boyfriend, Dion, and his buddy Matthaus said they'd be glad to help. Matthaus was sure that the road to Buffalo Creek and back would end between the sheets with Lisl. Both these guys had long criminal records. Lisl was virtually surrounded by losers.

They took two cars, Deme and Dion in one and Matthaus and Lisl in the other. In Buffalo Creek, the guys loaded up Lisl's stuff from her place, then used bolt cutters to pop the lock on the boyfriend's room to get some things that she had left in there. They also helped themselves to anything belonging to the boyfriend that they took a fancy to. The neighbors called the police; to them, it looked an awful lot like breaking and entering.

The cops caught up to Matthaus and Lisl on their way back to the city. A high-speed chase and running gun battle ensued. It terminated at Deme's apartment building in Denver. Lisl was immediately taken into custody and a hundred city cops, including riot and SWAT teams, cornered Jachnig in an exterior stairwell. When the smoke cleared, both Officer VanderJagt and Jachnig were dead. VanderJagt had been hit by ten rounds fired by three different weapons. Three rounds in the back. Jachnig had taken his own life with VanderJagt's gun.

If Matthaus Jachnig hadn't killed himself, Lisl would have been a witness for the prosecution and probably considered another victim. That wasn't the case. Instead, she was immediately charged with crimes associated with the break-in and the car chase. After a couple of days, some of the officers involved modified their statements and Lisl was charged with "felony murder." The "felony murder" statute allows for everyone involved in a felony to be charged with murder if a death results from the commission of the felony. The felony was the skinheads breaking into the boyfriend's apartment. I guess Deme and Dion weren't charged because they weren't part of the car chase, and one bullshit prosecution was enough.

Denver district attorney Bill Ritter offered a plea bargain. Auman would plead guilty to a reduced charge and would get thirty years, out in eighteen. Lisle's court-appointed attorney didn't bite. Lisl was innocent, and the attorney couldn't imagine that any jury would convict her. Everyone misjudged the depth of emotion running through the community. Lisl was convicted, and that was that. She sat in the state pen, without hope, until the day she wrote Hunter.

After her conviction, Lisl's mother and stepfather set up a website, www.lisl.com. It was all they could do. There was no way they could afford the kind of retainer that was demanded by the high-profile lawyers that they considered to be their only hope. Building a website and waiting for a miracle were all that their budget allowed.

They got their miracle.

About a month after Hunter and Lisl's exchange of letters, I was sitting in the kitchen with Doc while he worked on his ESPN column. He was somehow working Lisl Auman into a sports piece. It seemed pretty powerful to me, but I left well before it was finished, as Doc worked deep into the night. Once the article appeared on ESPN.com, the hits on the Lisl website began to swell to a thousand at a time. Lisl's parents thought there was a malfunction somewhere. Meanwhile, back in the Owl Farm kitchen, mixed reviews were coming in. The wacky crowd at ESPN were under the impression that they were in the sports business, not the girl-unjustly-jailed business. Ticked off is what they were. They didn't hesitate to read Hunter the riot act, something about using his column for his own personal agenda. Hunter was a bit sheepish about it, but he was used to pissing off his bosses.

In his response to Lisl, Hunter had promised he would look into her situation. The more he looked into it, the more he hated it. As it happened, the National Association of Criminal Defense Lawyers was meeting in Aspen that February. Their time in town coincided with Super Bowl Sunday. Hunter already knew a lot of the top defense lawyers in the country and he invited a bunch of them over for the game. I'm pretty sure that it was the weirdest Super Bowl I ever attended at Owl Farm. When the lawyers outnumber the dirtbags, the dirtbags get a bit uncomfortable. At half time, Hunter herded the lawyers into the living room and buried them with a pile of paperwork and documents. He assaulted them with their moral obligations. He bullied them with injustice. By the end of the game a lot of very important mouthpieces had signed on to Lisl's cause. Hunter was rallying the troops.

Next came a huge piece by Jeff Kass in the Sunday *Rocky Mountain News*. Jeff was a good friend, a good reporter, and a good soldier for the cause. His article seemed to take up most of the paper that day, and it couldn't help but get people's attention. One of those people was Matt Moseley. Matt was (and is) a senior associate at a public affairs firm GBSM, in Denver. He'd also done communications strategy for Rock the Vote, President Bill Clinton, the Olympics, and the Democrats at the Colorado State Capitol, among others. Matt had never met Hunter, but faxed him a memo outlining a public-information campaign about Lisl. Hunter called him back the same day. "Matt, this is

Hunter Thompson. Yeah. Uh, thanks for your memo." The two men, heretofore strangers, spoke for twenty-five minutes. The conversation concluded with "Hot damn, let's pull the trigger. Let's do a rally."

Matt proceeded to organize an event using as many of Hunter's connections as he could on short notice. Warren Zevon would be there; he'd sing "Lawyers, Guns and Money." Former head of the National Association of Criminal Defense Lawyers Gerry Goldstein would attend. Dottie Lamm, wife of former Colorado governor Dick Lamm, would also be there, along with presidential historian Doug Brinkley and astrophysics writer Timothy Ferris. The rally took place on the steps of the Colorado State Capitol and drew throngs of cheering fans.

At one point during the rally, Matt watched Hunter scribble, "Today's pig is tomorrow's bacon" on a notepad. Oh no, Matt thought, he can't say that. They were surrounded by cops keeping a very close watch on the proceedings. Matt leaned over to Hunter and suggested that it might not be the best-advised comment at that time. Hunter snapped back with "Don't tell me what to say."

Matt's favorite Hunter line is "There is no such thing as paranoia. It's always worse than you think." After the rally, Matt was escorting Hunter through the capitol to a loosely configured motorcade waiting on the south steps. A whole slew of people were crowding them and shouting. Matt was getting nervous, and Hunter could sense it. A photographer snapped a picture just as Hunter pulled on Matt's elbow and whispered into his ear, "Watch out for the assassins."

By 2003, when Hunter brought the Lisl Aumen case to the attention of *Vanity Fair* contributing editor Mark Seal, the machine had been grinding on for two years. We're all entitled to a speedy trial, but once convicted, the only people in a hurry are the incarcerated and their allies. The system itself feels that the job is done. Good luck getting it to hurry up and reverse itself. Mark was immediately struck by the obvious injustice of the case, as pointed out by Hunter. So Mark Seal came aboard, and the process crawled forward. There was to be a major article in *V.F.* It would be the first and last time Hunter coauthored anything.

Mark met Hunter in 2002 while doing a *Vanity Fair* piece on Aspen. He owned a home in town, and when they hooked up for the Lisl Auman article, Hunter's kitchen became the command post. This was when Seal became acquainted with Hunter's funny habit of calling at three or four in the morning: prime working hours for the Doctor, prime putting-up-with-Hunter hours for everyone else. To say they coauthored the article is being generous to Hunter. Hunter kept the drumbeat of activism rolling while Mark did the exhaustive research that was the meat of the piece. Ralph Steadman was commissioned to illustrate. His art struck to the heart of the revulsion that people felt about the case. Everyone was optimistic that the national spotlight of an article in *Vanity Fair* would create a breakthrough. Mark researched and wrote, fielding phone calls from Hunter in the wee hours. Ralph illustrated from England, fielding faxes from Woody Creek. Hunter coordinated, called, and faxed from his chair behind the counter in the kitchen.

When the article was finished, it was Hunter's turn. Mark had written the whole thing, and all Hunter had to do was write a lead, to get it started, and then wrap it up in the end. Seemed simple enough. Unfortunately Hunter was blocked. Really, really blocked. Considering how passionate he was about the subject, it was remarkable that he was having this problem.

There were deadlines; everything was ready to go, everything but Hunter. I'd be over there night after night. Voices would come on the speakerphone, mostly Mark's. "How's it going?" How was it going? It wasn't. "Oh, it's coming," would be the reply. This was important shit. The little girl in jail, the big-time magazine, all Mark Seal's work sitting, waiting for a beginning and an end. I don't know if Hunter would ask me over as a catalyst to try to get him working or as an excuse not to work. I'd always offer to leave if it was time for him to get down to it. On other projects he wouldn't hesitate to send me away so he could get stuff done. Unfortunately, there wasn't much of that going on at this point.

Finally, one evening, it seemed that things were approaching critical mass. Hunter and I were actually having a pretty good time, but there was a sense of urgency in the air of the kitchen. There was yet another phone call inquiring about progress. I excused myself; I said I had to run home for a second. When I returned, I brought a painting that I'd been working on for months. I was working from a vintage photograph of twenty-seven miners lined up in rows in front of a sawmill in Lenado, a ghost town a few miles up the road. The painting wasn't finished. I suggested that if Hunter was having a problem getting to work on his writing, he might want to take a crack at this goddamn thing, because it was driving me crazy. Hunter got the point, and I think he was glad that someone understood what he was going through, at least on some level. When I left, Hunter asked me to leave the painting. I briefly thought, Who cares if he writes this thing? Maybe he'll buy the painting. No such luck. That's what I get for being a selfish prick. The good news was that when I returned a couple of nights later, the article was finished, the crisis over, as if it had never happened.

I don't for a second think that my painting analogy did the trick. I suspect that the grumbling, and putting off the work, eventually became more work than actually doing the work.

"Prisoner of Denver," by Hunter Thompson and Mark Seal, illustrated by Ralph Steadman, appeared in the June 2004 issue of *Vanity Fair*. Hunter's introduction to the article was a vicious attack on the Denver law enforcement establishment, particularly District Attorney Bill Ritter and the Denver cops. They didn't take kindly to the piece, and at that point I wouldn't have taken a field trip to Denver with Hunter for love or money. At first they tried to be dismissive of the crackpot writer up in Woody Creek, but it was just about impossible to conceal their rage. Denver police chief Gerry Whitman described the piece as a "smear campaign" and said, "Thompson is not letting the facts stand in the way of a sensational attempt at journalism." But Mark's detailed research and extensive interviews laid bare the facts, and no amount of spin from the cops or the D.A. could change them.

The article gave the Free Lisl campaign a much-needed shot of adrenaline. In 2002 the Colorado Court of Appeals had refused to overturn the conviction, and that had slowed momentum a bit. The article validated people's involvement, particularly the high-profile Hollywood types like Sean Penn, Johnny Depp, and Benecio Del Toro. The next, and possibly last, step was the Colorado Supreme Court. Over the next few months the wheels kept turning at their own pace.

Then Hunter was gone. A month after his death, in March 2005, the Colorado Supreme Court decided that the Auman jury had been improperly instructed on the related burglary charge and ordered a new trial. The district attorney's office was dubious about its chances with another trial: "people's memories fade."

They agreed to a bargain. On October 17, 2005, Lisl Auman was released to Community Corrections. She spent Christmas with her family for the first time in eight years.

Posted on the Web site www.lisl.com:

Peace to Hunter S. Thompson.

Our Thoughts are with you Anita, and Jennifer, Juan and Will.

We would like to express our deepest sympathy to the Thompson family at the loss of Hunter.

We are grateful for his empathy and willingness to join in the effort to free Lisl from prison. As our friend, mentor and ally, he sustained and encouraged our family and Lisl's supporters. His energy, advice and knowledge were invaluable and seminal as we brought her case to the attention of our community and the world. He opened doors to opportunities which we would not have thought possible.

We hope and trust that his efforts on Lisl's behalf will be rewarded when the justice for which he strove will be served and she is set free.

God Bless you Hunter. You will be greatly missed.

—Don and Jeannette Auman and Rob and Colleen Auerbach

The Sheriff Investigates the Shooting of Deb

It was 7:00 A.M. I was in the shower when my wife, Louisa, announced that Hunter was on the phone and that he sounded upset. He wanted to talk to me immediately. I asked her to tell him that I would call him back post-shower. Seven in the morning was a very unusual time for a call from Hunter. Two, three, even four in the morning were normal—for Hunter. Most of the time these calls were answered by my voice-mail. Hunter's messages could ramble from five to forty minutes. I wish I had saved them all.

Three minutes later, Louisa came back to the shower and announced that Hunter had called back and was in a panic. He wanted to speak with me RIGHT NOW! While drying off, I took the portable phone. Our conversation was fast and furious: "Hunter, what's going on?" "I just shot Deborah. Come to Owl Farm now." "What? You just shot Deb?" "It was an accident. I was trying to scare away a bear. Get over here." "Where is Deb now?" "She's at the hospital." "Hunter, I'm going over there first. I'll call you later."

In Colorado, medical facilities are legally required to report stabbings, gunshot wounds, and dog bites to law enforcement agencies. When I arrived at the emergency room, two deputies were already there. Scott Thompson, patrol director, and Joey DiSalvo, my director of investigations, briefed me and led me to Deborah Fuller, one of my personal heroines. She had been working for Hunter for close to twenty years. Deb was lying on a gurney, and when she saw me she said, "Bobby, how's Hunter?" I told her that he'd called asking me to come to Owl Farm but that her condition was more important right now. She showed me a half-dozen wounds, some with visible birdshot pellets just below the skin. The initial examination and X-rays showed "flesh wounds" with no deep penetration. Deborah's mood was stoic; she was smiling and still had her ironic sense of humor. "Hunter has threatened to shoot me dozens of times, and now the son-of-a-bitch has!" She was laughing.

Deborah asked me to stay when the doctor explained his suggested treatment. Basically, he told Deb that surgical removal of the number six lead pellets would be intrusive and posed a risk of infection and a host of other risks, as with any procedure of that nature. He described the risk of lead poisoning as minimal. Without much hesitation, Deb decided against the scalpel—and, again, asked me how Hunter was handling this event.

Hunter was an aficionado of firearms. From handguns to shotguns and rifles (both sporting and assault), many targets have been hit, missed, or blown up at the Woody Creek Rod and Gun Club, also know as Owl Farm. The "club" was incorporated in the early seventies, shortly after Hunter was informed of George Stranahan's plan to open the Aspen Community School next door. The Doc didn't miss many tricks and was aware that certain activities, including the discharge of firearms, were legally verboten anywhere near a school. His lawyers advised him that his "club' would enjoy grandfather status relative to the planned school and would be permitted to coexist with his new neighbor. Over the years, and hundred of thousands of discharged cartridges later, Hunter's safety record was sterling. Until now.

Satisfied with Deb's medical stability, my deputy sheriffs took their notes from an interview with her and left victim/witness forms to be completed at her convenience. We left the hospital and drove to the "crime scene." All assaults were considered criminal until they were investigated and underwent prosecutorial review. The three of us arrived at Owl Farm and were greeted by Hunter. Joey requested a consent-to-search, in writing, from Hunter. After inquiring about Deb's condition, Hunter told us that he felt the need to run past one of his many lawyers our request to search the premises. We explained that he had that right, but if he decided to refuse his consent, we would have to swear out an affidavit and application for a search warrant issued by a judge.

Hunter called the office of Abe Hutt, one of Denver's best and brightest in the arena of criminal defense. When Abe's secretary said that Abe was in court, Hunter acquiesced and signed the consent. (Weeks later, Abe, a friend of mine, confided to me that if he had been contacted by Hunter, his advice would have been to require us to get a warrant.) Scott gathered evidence, photographed the scene, took measurements, and documented the forensic elements. Joey and I, after delivering the required Miranda advisement, asked Hunter what had happened.

Deborah lived in a two-bedroom cabin about thirty yards from Hunter's house. The area had been experiencing a multi-year drought and some late-season frosts, both of which had greatly reduced the natural food supply of the black bear, a regular and long-term resident of Woody Creek. Adapting to changes in their environment, the bears found almost unlimited alternative sources of sustenance, primarily in trash cans and Dumpsters laden with leftovers awaiting removal by garbage trucks. Hunter's domestic trash was in a Dumpster midway between his house and Deborah's cabin. He recounted that on this morning, in the murky light of dawn, he peered out a window and saw a large beast loitering just outside of Deborah's door. He phoned to warn her and got the answering machine. Assuming that she was still sound asleep, he decided to do what he had done in many previous encounters with trespassing wildlife. He loaded a small-gauge shotgun with two shells filled with number-six birdshot. Each piece of shot was somewhere between the size of a BB and a poppy seed. With no desire to wound the animal, Hunter aimed at the gravel on the driveway several feet short of the bear. Generally the noise and the resulting launch of gravel toward the target spooked ursine intruders into a rapid exit.

Hunter labeled this technique the "bounce shot" and expressed pride in his accuracy with it. "Tell that to Deborah," suggested DiSalvo. That morning, according to Hunter, just as he pulled the trigger, Deborah opened her screen door and ended up directly behind the bear.

Scott, Joey, and I left Owl Farm with cartridges, the shotgun, some pellets dug out of Deborah's door, and photographs. Interview notes to be entered into official reports, ranges and vectors to be diagrammed and analyzed, and the provision of a witness statement were the job of Scott and Joe.

The media were salivating, and we wrote a preliminary press release that emphasized that the case was open and under investigation. I had been criticized for years by a small minority of citizens for continuing my friendship with a self-proclaimed dope fiend and random brat. My agency had, in the past, investigated certain allegations of Hunter's reckless behavior, dangerous or criminal. In a few of these cases I had called in outside agencies to assume investigative responsibilities. At one point, in frustration, I told Hunter I could be his friend or his sheriff but not always both at the same time. He understood. He always asserted his innocence and never apologized or explained, but he did offer that he didn't do crazy shit unless he could write about it and get paid. This day's incident was an exception. I accepted the risk of the situation and still feel that I was fair to my duties and fair to my friend.

While those deputies qualified to put together the evidence and statements were doing their work, the wire services and print media, as well as the TV news hounds, were already beating their drums. "Thompson shoots long-time assistant" was the headline in America and many foreign countries. I needed advice from the district attorney.

Over the years, Hunter had been investigated by the current DA, Mac Myers, and by Mac's predecessor. Mac had worked for the previous DA, Milt Blakey, who loathed Hunter. At one point, Mac had decided to enter private practice as a defense attorney and resigned as deputy DA. As a career prosecutor, he wanted to look at his life's profession from the other side of the street. Eventually he made the decision to represent the people of the State of Colorado and challenged his former boss in the 1996 election. Mac, a Democrat, defeated Blakey in a largely right-wing Republican district.

At noon on the day of the Fuller shooting, I called Mac, who had not heard anything of the morning's events. "Mac, Braudis here. Got a minute?" "Sure, what's up?" "Let me run a hypothetical by you." "Sure, go ahead." "Okay, a guy looks out of his house and sees a black bear hanging around just outside of the door of his guest house. He attempts to warn the guest but gets the answering machine. He assumes that the guest is still asleep and, concerned for her safety, decides to use a technique to run off the bear that has been successful in the past." I described the elements of the "bounce shot." "Just as he fired the shotgun," I continued, "the guest opens the door and is hit by some of the birdshot. Her injuries are minor. She has unequivocally asserted her desire not to prosecute or even sue for negligent behavior. We have conducted a complete investigation including statements, a signed consent-to-search, and all the physical evidence. Mac, crime or no crime?" I asked.

"Well, it could be marginal, and I emphasize marginal, criminal endangerment. But given what you have told me, and assuming that it is true, I call it an accident. Sort of like falling off the roof."

"Okay Mac, here's the kicker," I said. "The bounce shot defender of guests is Hunter."

"Oh, shit," Mac responded. "Can you get down to my office with all the reports, photos, diagrams, evidence, and Joey later today?"

Joey and I met with Mac that afternoon and we exchanged expressions of exasperation mixed with humor and relief that a very good friend had escaped serious injury. Mac agreed to review the case and touch base with Deborah as soon as possible.

He said that he would issue a press release when he had reached a decision. At noon the following day, the office of the Ninth Judicial District Attorney issued a press release that exonerated the Doc from any criminal charges. The tabloids and sensational journalists got a few more days' play. Hunter got a lecture from me, ranging from condemning cavalier reliance upon firearms to suggesting alternatives to "bounce-shooting" in the interest of bear mitigation. Cables and locking snaps were added to the Dumpster. Hunter remained my friend, and I remained his sheriff. I gained even more respect for Deborah, for her class and loyalty, which formed part of the currency in the constant potential for nightmare in her relationship with HST.

I remained his sheriff.

P.S. CLEVERLY

Of course all of this was big news in Woody Creek, the talk of the Tavern. I don't think it was a coincidence that Hunter stayed away for several days. I doubt that he would ever have admitted it, but I suspect he was embarrassed. We all loved Deborah, and even Hunter wasn't immune to the Tavern sense of humor.

A couple nights after the "incident," I heard a commotion in my backyard. I opened the door to find a small black bear; I hollered and shooed him off. I called Owl Farm. I didn't know how the legal situation was evolving with the Sheriff's Department, or even Fish and Game. Since my cabin is less than a mile from Hunter's I wanted to be able to back his play regarding the actual existence of a marauding bear. Hunter answered, and I told him all of this. "Where's the bear now?" he asked. "Gone" I said, "and no one got hurt." Hunter was pissed at me for a while.

Cleverly Faces Fans Gone Wild

The call came in the middle of a sunny summer afternoon. "Michael, you have to get over here. There's been a security breach!" This is the sort of message I'd usually get on my answering machine at three in the morning. At 3:15, when the message ended, I'd pull my fingers out of my ears, roll over, and go back to sleep. It was different this time. Perhaps there was something to it. I asked Hunter what was going on. "Just get over here right now. This is important." I could tell that he meant it. "Here I come." I eyeballed the sawed-off shotgun on the wall. Nah. Far too pretty a day for that kind of solution, no matter how bad the situation.

There's a long history of fans coming to Woody Creek in search of Hunter. One day I was called to the Tavern to check out a guy who claimed to be a filmmaker needing directions to Owl Farm. It took about a minute to size him up and decide that the term *would-be* should precede anything he claimed to be. He was alone, no crew, and his camera was about the size of a cell phone—maybe it was a cell phone. It looked pretty silly sitting on top of this large, professional-type tripod. I told him Hunter was sleeping, which might have been true, and that if he didn't have an invitation, which I knew he didn't, there was no way he was going to get into Owl Farm. He complained that he had been on his way to the "Burning Man" festival and that he had driven a thousand miles out of his way to meet Hunter. I told him that was his problem and to go away. He asked if he could interview me. I said no and split. When I got home I left a message of warning on Hunter's machine. The guy ended up finding his way to Owl Farm anyway and stole a liquor delivery and some dry cleaning that had been left on Hunter's porch. A loving gesture by a devoted fan.

On another occasion a young fella got a job as a busboy at the Tavern. This may or may not have been a gambit to get close to Hunter. He was a nice clean-cut kid who wanted to be a writer, and if it was a ploy, it wasn't a bad one. Hunter was always as decent to Tavern employees as his mood allowed, and in some way they were instantly part of the family. The kid was bright and drove an old beater motorcycle, so if he'd been patient and bided his time I suspect he and Hunter could have hooked up cordially. Unfortunately it wasn't to be. He got himself completely shitfaced one night and made his way up to Owl Farm. Hunter had no idea who he was, and there was no way it could have ended well anyway. In this particular case, it was a warm summer night and the Shark was parked in the driveway with the top down; puking in it was no way to get on Hunter's good side. The kid's tenure at the Tavern didn't last long.

To my way of thinking there were three distinct types of people who would come to visit Hunter uninvited, all of them fans, of course.

There were those who actually understood that it was a bit odd to travel a great distance to impose themselves on someone they'd never met. This category of fan was a little embarrassed and maybe a little puzzled by their own behavior. I found these people to be generally benign and I always tried to treat them gently and with a measure of courtesy.

Then there were those whose judgment was impaired; you know, whacked, loaded, a bit fucked up. These folks would probably be fine the next day, but at the time, they weren't very pleasant company. They usually were sure they were right and were often belligerent. One tried to reason with them, to make them go away. It wasn't an easy project. Those situations would often end up with people with badges getting involved.

Then there were the true nutcases. Sober or straight, they would wake up one morning and decide that it was a perfectly reasonable idea to drive (or hitchhike or teleport) themselves thousands of miles and drop in on someone they'd never laid eyes on. These types were convinced that because they'd traveled all that way, Hunter owed them something—despite the fact that no one had asked them to come or wanted them there. If they couldn't find Hunter, then Hunter's friends, employees, or family owed them something. Those were my favorites. They didn't sober up the next day. They rarely took no for an answer.

So, on this particular sunny afternoon, guess what sort of person had driven himself off the road across from Hunter's driveway.

I had noticed a pair of black tire marks heading toward the pasture across from Doc's the day before. The pasture was home to alpacas, llamas, guinea fowl, turkeys, and God knows what else. The black tire marks suggested to me that someone had come to a screeching halt inches before crashing through the fence that kept the critters where they belonged. I got a feeling that I was about to meet the author of those tire marks.

When I got there, Deborah was leaning into the passenger-side window of a car that seemed to have stopped just short of rolling over. The fact that it was deep in a ditch and almost on its side actually made Deborah's position quite comfortable. I pulled my Jeep across the entrance to Hunter's driveway, effectively blocking anyone from pulling in or out. As I stepped out of the Jeep, Deborah pulled her head out of the car window. Michael, I'd like you to meet so and so. So and so, meet Michael. Michael's a good friend of Hunter's. Deborah's tone was casual and gracious, as if she were introducing people at a cocktail party. This wasn't her first crazy person. I took up Deborah's head-in-window position and said hello.

The inside of the guy's car looked like what I presumed the inside of his head must have looked like. It was a goddamn mess. There was shit everywhere. Not just the usual slob debris. There were strange devices; perhaps he used them to talk to the "voices." I motioned for Deborah to back up and suggested that she go inside and tell Hunter that I was here. I wanted her out of the line of fire, should there be a line of fire. He was a good-size lad. I realized that this wasn't our first meeting. He'd been at the Tavern the day before. A great big kid sitting at the end of the bar, brooding and asking about Hunter. Well, there we were.

I proceeded with some small talk. He wasn't making much sense, but I didn't get the feeling that he was loaded. We continued to chat; it all seemed affable enough. I thought that things were going well; then I noticed a beater pickup truck heading toward us at a high rate of speed. Tex. Evidently, Hunter had called Tex and me at the same time. I lived a little closer and got there first. The vehicle approached and Tex slammed on the brakes, skidding sideways in our direction. Tex was out of the truck almost before it stopped moving. He had a lever-action carbine in his hand. Clearly he had come to a different conclusion than I had when he eyeballed his arsenal on the way out of the house.

He ran full speed to the car and stuck the rifle in the kid's face. I was pretty sure that this was running counter to my chilling-the-kid-out strategy. I told Tex that I thought I had things covered and that maybe he should go establish a perimeter. Reluctantly he withdrew the weapon. Tex melted into the scenery. I went back to trying to re-chill the kid.

A few minutes later, Doug Brinkley walked down the driveway and stopped in the middle of the road. Doug was a dear friend of Doc's. He had been very helpful to him on a number of projects and happened to be visiting that afternoon. Doug is a presidential historian and a Jimmy Carter and Rosa Parks biographer. Doug is on TV a lot for CBS News. I could think of any number of accurate phrases to describe Doug but "up from the streets" wouldn't be one of them. "Camera ready" would be more like it. Doug had an affinity for starched white shirts.

I pulled my head out of the car window and met up with Doug in the middle of the road. Just as I got there, a guy on a bicycle came down the road. He stopped and told us that on his way up the road this guy had forced him off the road and into a ditch. Hmmm, just the kind of thing that Hunter would have seriously considered doing. Maybe the kid was all right. The bicyclist told us that he had called the cops. Damn cell phones. No one's safe from the decent citizenry. I told Doug that everything was fine and suggested he go inside. The bike guy pedaled off, and Doug went back up the driveway, relieved, I suspect. I stuck my head back inside the car and told the kid that he might have misbehaved and that the authorities had been summoned.

I explained that the sheriff was Hunter's friend and mine. I told him that Bob's people were out to do the right thing, not to see how many arrests they could make. Everything was going to be okay. I told him that in the spirit of cooperation and not getting into too deep shit, if he had any weapons in the vehicle it would be incredibly intelligent to pitch them out the window right now. I also mentioned that if he had any drugs in there, he should go ahead and give them to me. I saw the Sheriff's Department cruiser coming up the road. I soothed the kid as best I could.

The sheriff's boys pulled up in front of the kid's car, thus blocking the neighbor's driveway. Naturally, the neighbor drove up almost as soon as the deputies got out. He gave me the "what's going on?" look. I explained to the deputies that they were parked in this guy's driveway, and explained to the neighbor, who was in fact a rock-and-roll star, that he had a different sort of fan base than Hunter and should be glad of it. He understood instantly; the deputies let him pass. I introduced myself to the constabulary and introduced them to the kid. I handed off and excused myself knowing that things could have gone much worse.

I made my way up the driveway to the house and into the kitchen. Doug was there, Deborah, Tex, Anita, Hunter of course, and I think a couple of part-time assistants. As always, Hunter's gratitude was almost suffocating. "I'm sick of you people running in here and hiding behind me" were the first words that I heard from him. My distinct impression had been that people were running out the door in an effort to place themselves between

Hunter and the nut job. Realizing how wrong I must have been about that, I simply agreed with Hunter. "Okay, Doc, got to be going." I asked Tex if he was coming along, figuring that nothing but abuse could follow. Tex allowed that he was going to stay a bit and bask in the warmth of the moment.

Things were quiet in Woody Creek for the rest of the day.

It was midnight. I was shifting up through the gears on the entrance ramp to I-70 East, headed from Glenwood Springs to the Denver airport. We were trying to beat a blizzard that was likely to close DIA for another forty-eight hours just as one had done the week before.

Instead of leaving much earlier in the day and spending the night in a hotel near the airport, DeDe and I had dinner at Ed Bradley's house in Woody Creek. Ed had died forty-nine days before, and today was the Bardo, the day that his spirit would take residence in a new life form, according to Tibetan Buddhist beliefs. Ed's wife, Patricia, had arranged for monks to chant, burn incense, and help Ed's spirit to find its release. Later, she had a dinner party for close friends.

Hunter and Ed were very close. Hunter had brought Ed to Aspen, and Ed became a resident of Woody Creek. Two "journalists in residence," they shared an enthusiasm for fast cars and they are both gone now. I thought back to our adventures and the vehicles we drove.

Hunter and machines had always enjoyed a close relationship. The mobility of cars or motorcycles meant independence and freedom to him. Hunter felt trapped if he didn't control his mobility. On the road there was always a rental

Ed and Doc; one was more gonzo and one was more golf.

car parked close by, in case he wanted to disappear. If I drove him in his car (I hardly ever rode with him), he would ask for the keys as soon as I parked.

"Never lose control of your ride," he once told me as I handed him his key ring. "I've made that mistake a few times," he added. I could relate. Handing him his keys meant that suddenly I wasn't in control of my mobility.

Bradley called Hunter one morning and suggested that they fly to Denver to do some car shopping. Hunter had just acquired a (for that time) state-of-the-art video camera. He put this twenty-pound monster into a duffel bag, and off to Denver they went. The cab rides to a couple of car dealerships were recorded, as was the negotiation that concluded with Ed's ownership of a Porsche Carrera convertible. Ed, who had been a New York City guy for many years and not a car owner, couldn't get anywhere with insurance. Hunter, by phone with his agent in Aspen, got Ed a binder and they drove off the lot with Hunter videotaping. Hunter called the tape "Mr. Ed Goes to Market."

The trip home took them to Leadville, where sundry purchases were made and memorialized on video, and where Ed handed Hunter the keys to the Porsche. Hunter packed the camera into his duffel, adjusted the seat and mirrors, and headed toward Independence Pass, a narrow, winding mountain road over the Continental Divide to Aspen. The camera was in the bag with the lens cap on but was still running, recording audio. After several minutes of wind and road noise and banter, Ed could be heard saying, "Hunter, you might want to slow down a little." No response. "Hunter! This is a bad curve coming up, a thousand-foot drop-off! Slow down!" Hunter: "Don't worry, Ed. I'm a pro." Ed: "You motherfucker! You're gonna kill us. Slow down!"

Ed enjoying a peaceful evening with the Doctor and friends.

That's one of the reasons I never rode with Hunter. He took pleasure in scaring the hell out of people, and often did. But as is often the case with people who are good at dishing it out, he didn't take it well.

One night, returning to Woody Creek from Aspen, Hunter's next-door neighbor Ed Bastian was at the wheel, with Hunter in the backseat. Bastian declared that we were going to "run silent," meaning that he was turning off the headlights. As Ed wheeled his Ford Explorer through the curves on McLain Flats Road in total darkness, Hunter screamed from the back seat, "Ed! You're gonna kill us! Ed! For Christ's sake! What about people coming at us?" Boys at play. Ed in some small way getting even.

After a couple of years enjoying his Porsche convertible, Bradley pulled into the parking lot at the Woody Creek Tavern one summer evening. Hunter and I had just finished dinner and it was suggested that we go into town for drinks. I had my car, but HST wanted to ride into Aspen in the Shark. Ed said that he needed gas and followed us to Owl Farm.

We gassed both convertibles from Hunter's three-hundred-gallon tank, and Ed pulled out of the driveway first. Hunter and I were right behind, with me at the wheel of the Chevy. Hunter ordered me to pass Ed, but Ed wasn't going to be passed. Hunter was yelling at me to go faster as the Porsche disappeared from view. Porsche versus Chevy: Porsche wins. We arrived in Aspen and walked into the bar. Ed was sitting in the lounge and asked, "What took you so long? I'm on my second drink." Somehow I got stuck with that check.

In 1970, Hunter and I pulled out of Owl Farm and turned left on the dirt road to Lenado. We were both riding Bultaco Matadors, Spanish dirt bikes that were built for racing. I followed him up the road. He was comfortable in the seat and understood counter-steering and gyroscopic force. We were two of the few riders who appreciated this motorcycle designed by Señor Bulto; it was still superior to Japanese bikes. Hunter had logged a lot of miles on his BSA in California and on his BMW in Colorado. *Cycle World* magazine would arrange for him to test-ride motorcycles from Ducatis to Triumphs and write about them. Over the years to come, as his motor skills began to deteriorate, I began to worry about him on two wheels. Riding with him eventually became out of the question.

One day he called me at home and wanted to know what I was doing. I told him that I was about to have dinner with a bunch of friends and invited him over. We were on the back porch eating when we saw Hunter on his BMW riding through the next-door neighbor's backyard. He saw us and turned into my yard, lost control of his motorcycle, and fell. He was lying on the grass under the 750-cc bike with gasoline running from its tank and onto his chest. I lifted the giant motorcycle off him, gave him a clean shirt, and filled his drink order. I insisted that I drive him home after dinner. Two weeks later he called and asked if I could deliver his bike. I rode it to Owl Farm. The throttle stuck, and the brakes didn't work. I told him that the motorcycle was not safe, but I knew he was going to ride it again. I didn't want to think about it.

At one point, feeling the need of something big and bright red, Hunter bought himself a vintage Pontiac convertible. Not long after, the Mitchell Brothers, of O'Farrell Theater fame, came to Aspen in support of Hunter's defense against charges of assault by a retired porn star. With them the brothers had a 1970 Impala convertible, fully restored and fully red. It was to replace the Shark, which had played a prominent role in *Fear and Loathing in Las Vegas*. Hunter told me that he had hidden the Pontiac in the barn, and not to tell the Mitchell brothers about it; he was afraid that they might take the Chevy back. Soon after they left town, Hunter bought another convertible, a Cadillac, from his buddy Earl Biss, a crazy Crow Indian artist with a crack problem. Hunter couldn't get a good title to the car but he had it detailed anyway. He parked it on the lawn, side by side with the two other large trophy vehicles. Biss was proud that his ride was part of that collection.

One night I was in the kitchen with Hunter and Woody Creek lawyer John Van Ness. In the middle of our conversation, Earl walked in with a camel hair sport coat over his arm. With a grin, he said, "You white men are easy. I took a cab to your meadow, walked across to your house, let myself in, and I've been lying on your porch with my coat as a pillow listening to you talk for an hour." Earl had been practicing his Native American sneaking-up skills. "What do you want, Earl?" Hunter asked.

"Give me a forty-five. I want to kill myself" was Earl's reply.

"I have to go" Van Ness said as he put on his coat.

"You coward," Hunter said to Van Ness.

"Give me the gun," Biss demanded.

"You're crazy, Earl," Hunter said.

"Give him the gun, Hunter. Call his bluff," I said.

"You're crazy, too" Hunter said to me.

After a long silence that no one enjoyed, Earl started laughing like a hyena and said, "I don't know what I would have done if you had given me the gun."

Just another night in the kitchen.

On another day, Hunter pulled the freshly waxed and shampooed Cadillac, Geronimo's Cadillac, out of the row of cars and said, "Hop in. It's got front-wheel drive," as if that explained everything—or anything.

We headed toward the Woody Creek Racetrack, off-road all the way. Trying to climb a six-foot berm onto the racetrack, Hunter bogged the Eldorado down in rain-soaked dirt. The front wheels spun, and mud flew all over the car. Hunter, not to be defeated, asked me to place the spotless floor mats under the drive wheels. I did. Hunter gassed it, and the rugs flew into the sage. "Move over," I said to Hunter.

Turning the steering wheel lock to lock and shifting the transmission repeatedly from Drive to Reverse, I loosened the beast and drove it back to the farm. The car and I were covered in mud. Hunter hated to fail at anything and pouted all the way home.

"At least I stayed clean," he said to me as I pulled the filthy Cadillac into its space in the line.

Now it was 2:00 A.M. No snow yet, and we were halfway to Denver. We pulled into an all-night Denny's to take on some caffeine. It had been a long time since DeDe and I threaded a car through the night and I looked over the crowd here just off the Interstate and saw a bunch of people each with his or her own story.

I thought of Ed Bradley, Hunter, Earl, gone too, and us driving in the dark to catch the last plane out of the Rockies to the East Coast.

Sheriff Bob Relates Fun and Games at the Vail Clinic

After Hunter's hip replacement, which is another story, his spine was declared a Superfund site. Pain was his game. He would brag of his tolerance of it, tolerance assisted by all known and some unknown chemicals. When pain eclipsed his pharmacopoeia, the Doc went to the docs.

I had recently had spinal surgery, and Hunter asked for a referral. I was glad to help. My surgery had been a complete success. Tests, diagnosis, and good patient-surgeon chemistry resulted in Hunter having a "spine replacement," as Hunter told his friends.

The surgery, while complex and successful, led directly to a very difficult "withdrawal." Anita, Juan, and Deborah shared watches over the operation and the ensuing withdrawal. I would get updates they issued from the clinic in Vail. The essence of these dispatches was that the surgery was a technical success but that Hunter was suffering significantly. This had resulted in a decision to induce coma and to transfer the patient to the Intensive Care Unit, not because Hunter needed intensive care but because the unit had solid doors, which would protect the other patients from Hunter's screaming outbursts of rage when he briefly awoke from his enforced sleep.

Withdrawal is a phenomenon that most good hospitals have experience with. The Vail Clinic had seen its share of patients with hooch complications. A 5 percent, ten-proof IV solution works in most cases. The MDs told me that 5 percent was not enough with this particular patient, but that rules were rules. They also told me that it was not merely the alcohol that was causing Hunter's problems. A list of drugs, many unknown to me, were blamed for the "kick." Pills in all shapes and sizes were the cause of my friend's hinky freak-outs. The coma was not induced merely because of alcohol, but so what? Cleanse the man.

Two weeks after the surgery I was sitting in my office when Doc called. He wanted me to be his first visitor outside the family. I agreed to drive to Vail over the next two hours. I walked into the hospital and was immediately routed to the ICU Deb had already warned me the IV wasn't working. I had brought a bottle of port that I knew HST liked. What I didn't know was that the feeding tube—critical while Hunter was in a coma, but now removed—had made swallowing an Olympic event. I poured a glass of port, hoping to alleviate at least part of the withdrawal pain. HST thanked me and lifted the glass to his lips. He dropped it and it shattered on the hospital floor. What next?

Hunter ordered Juan, Anita, and Deborah from the room. He raved to me that Juan only wanted his money, that Anita was depressed that she was the wife, nurse, housekeeper, editorial assistant, and future widow of an old and decrepit journalist who believed that he was soon to expire or require 24-7 care. Now it was me, HST, and his beautiful blond nurse. Hunter whispered in my ear, "Get me out of here!" I replied "Spring you?" Hunter said, "No, take me to a bar." I told the nurse that the Doc wanted me to take him to a bar. She said it was against doctor's orders but it would probably do him a world of good.

Okay.

The wheelchair-bound Hunter asked to be dressed in scrubs like the nurse. She agreed, and we dressed him. No small task: spinal surgery, chemically induced coma, his first visitor, a sympathetic RN.

I lifted him while the nurse garbed him in scrubs. The nurse gave HST an injection in the thigh. "What's that?" I asked. "Haldol" was her answer. "Haldol? Jesus, we use that in my jail on psychotic inmates. It's a chemical Rip Van Winkle. He'll be a noodle in a chair with wheels, with me in charge." "It's a very small dose," she replied. "Hot damn!" the Doc exclaimed. "Let's go!"

I pushed him out onto the streets of Vail. In a car with suspension and shocks, these streets feel and look like glass. Now two voyagers on foot and wheel going uphill, we found the road pocked with potholes. It was ninety degrees, and I was sweating like a lord. HST was vibrating in the wheelchair like an astronaut just after liftoff. His voice was in tremolo, and his teeth were chattering.

The first liquor license that we came to was fortunately ADA-compliant. A three-switchback ramp led to an outdoor patio with umbrella tables. "Want to sit outside?" I asked, assuming that two weeks indoors at a hospital would have Hunter yearning for sunshine. I forgot the Doc's vampire syndrome; he feared sunlight. "No, let's go inside." Once we were settled at a table inside, Hunter lit up a Dunhill. Instantly, a ponytailed waiter materialized and announced, "There's no smoking here." I took over. "Look, dude, the guys been in the hospital for weeks, and this is his first cigarette." I simultaneously peeled a twenty from my wad and offered the mordida. Ponytail looked left and right, swished the twenty from my fingers like a snapping turtle, and returned with an ashtray. We ordered drinks. After the delivery of HST's Chivas and my gin and tonic, Hunter pulled out a pipe and a Bic. Shit. Well, in for a penny . . .

But before he could light the pipe, his chin was on his chest. He was nodding. Jesus. "Hunter! Hunter!" He lifted his head and met my eyes.

"Want to go back?"

"Yeah. Better take me back."

I overpaid for the untouched cocktails and started pushing the chair. HST was slumping farther forward, and I feared that he was going to fall on his face. I grabbed him by the collar of his surgical scrubs. The chair had a seat belt, and I cinched him up just before total unconsciousness descended. Back inside the hospital, six of us used a blanket to gently return Hunter to his crib. He was snoring. I drove back to Aspen.

At about eight o'clock that night I was dining in Woody Creek at the home of a friend. My cell phone lit up. It was Anita calling. "Bobby, I'm in the valley following a limo that has Hunter in it. He called it to drive him home from Vail. I may need some help getting him into the house." I told her I was five minutes away and to call when they got to the house. She phoned a little later and said that with the help of the driver and Cleverly, Hunter was back at Owl Farm and grinning.

After weeks of physical therapy, stretching, and a commitment to mobility, Hunter was recovering from a major overhaul that he could barely recall. We all celebrated his return and did what we could to support him physically, mentally, and intellectually. Reflecting on his accepting the necessity of the surgery and the inherent pain, before and after the procedure, reinforced my belief that Hunter wanted more out of life—or at least, more life.

When he asked me to ride with him in his Jeep Grand Cherokee a few days after his return, I balked, but he convinced me that it would be a short test-drive in his quest for eventual automotive independence. He promised to stay on Owl Farm property. Against my better judgment, I got the car from the garage. He groped his way to the driver's door, hand over hand on the roof rack, and into the seat. I got in beside him, and he put it in drive. With feet numb from the days in bed and spinal swelling, he floored the accelerator. Wheels spinning, we bounced into the large field behind the house. He could press down on the accelerator, steer, jump two-foot logs, and mow down fence posts, but somehow he just could not move his right foot to the brake pedal. We careened over a pile of rotting cottonwood logs, through a wire sheep fence, and across two irrigation ditches before I could reach over and turn off the engine. I yanked the keys out of the ignition. "Switch seats or stay here as long as you want!" I bellowed. He grinned, thanked me, and complied with my order. "Mission accomplished," he said with a smile.

I drove back very slowly, recovering from my terror and let him out at the house. I parked the car back in the garage and gave Anita the keys and told her it would be a while before the Doc could drive. It was.

Bob Describes a Mishap on Assignment

I told Hunter not to go to Honolulu. He'd been invited there to be the celebrity host for a marathon on Oahu, but he was still recovering from spinal surgery. His gait was unsteady and unbalanced. Hobbling from the kitchen to the bathroom was a fifteen-minute round trip. I often watched him discreetly piss in the kitchen sink with his back to the crowd in order to avoid the trek. Sometimes he asked me to stand behind him as a human cloak. Oh yeah, you gotta love the stench of urine on dirty dishes. Juan, much later, confided that his father had done this even when he was healthy.

Nonetheless, the packing of suitcases commenced. Five-star digs, Pacific Rim hero worshipers, Gollywood stablemates, sun instead of ice, wanderlust, and grins trumped my Jesuit logic and intuitive concern that argued against this postsurgical maiden voyage of Hunter, the shipwreck that I loved and worried about. His medical crusade was boring and draining, and respite was worth the gamble. And gambling man he was. An audience broader than the kitchen, a reaffirmation of his cachet, and the challenge to show us that transoceanic travel was still an arrow in his quiver kicked him into gear and he spurred his gang of sherpas onward. In the end, paranoia was the only serious threat to his journey, and paranoia lost out. With baggage more properly suited to a nineteenth-century steamship circumnavigation, Mr. and Mrs. Thompson left for the islands.

The first phone call evoked a flood of "why didn't I put my foot down?" guilt. Hunter had snapped both tibia and fibula, just below the knee, in a slip-and-fall on the marble floor of his tropical paradise bathroom and he was being put back together and encased in plaster in the orthopedic section of the Honolulu Valley Hospital. Setback? Understatement.

I like facts. I like to garner facts. The facts are neither sad nor happy, they just exist.

Hunter wanted a microwave oven in his suite. The major counter space was in the bathroom, with deluxe slick marble floors. At some ungodly hour of predawn, Hunter craved Top Ramen soup. He nuked it, reached into the oven for it, grabbed it, burned his hand on it, dropped it on the floor, took a step, went upside down, landed without grace, snapped two bones, and never got any soup. Just the facts, ma'am.

Anita provided the play-by-play. "Bobby, we're flying Honolulu to DIA, then to Vail and the Steadman clinic. I'll call you from there." But Anita's next call came from Honolulu. She recounted the checking of baggage, pre-boarding the United jumbo, first-class seats, row 1, A and B, Hunter's failure to find comfort and his insistence on deplaning. Post-9/11 stomach acid for UAL and TSA. The baggage went round trip to Denver and back.

A few days later, Anita, thinking logically, booked six seats in the center section of a wide body. Hunter could lie down and find comfort. One problem, the FAA says you cannot lie down during takeoff and landing. Scratch plan B. Plan C was an air ambulance dispatched from L.A. and guaranteed by Sean Penn's Gold Card. The flight crew loaded Hunter and Anita aboard the jet and headed east toward the Vail airport and the Steadman-Hawkins Clinic.

There was trouble mid-Pacific. Hunter was not comfortable and chucked water bottles and sandwiches into the cockpit. That sort of thing is verboten in the world of Learjet jockeys; those guys aren't used to having stuff thrown at them in mid-flight. At a scheduled refueling stop at Van Nuys, the crew told Anita that Hunter was going to be dumped out of his stretcher on to the tarmac for his horrible behavior. He could find his own way to Vail. Anita begged the crew to relent. The pilots took pity, and the flight continued.

Meanwhile, I was on the phone with Juan, who was en route to Vail. I said I'd meet him at the clinic. Anita had been up for five days and once Hunter was settled in at Steadman-Hawkins, she checked into a ski lodge for a well-deserved nap. I met Juan in the clinic lobby. You could hear Hunter clear down the hall, and it was agonizing. Acknowledging that the goal was to get Hunter to Owl Farm when the orthos were done assessing his condition, Juan, with a real life and a real job and a very real family, sought my permission to return to Denver. I would stand watch and coordinate from Vail to the farm. There was no sense in both of us watching NFL games in the lobby all Sunday afternoon.

Juan gave me the phone numbers of Anita's lodge and a limo service and went back to Denver. The staff at the clinic told me that X-rays of Doc's break showed clean fractures, no dislocation and no need for surgery or admission. They sedated him and recast his leg from ass to toe with thirty pounds of plaster. Later, during the second games of the afternoon, I was told by the staff that Hunter was ready to go, and that they were ready for him to leave. Those who had to attend to him would shed no tears. He would not be missed. As he emerged from anesthesia I could hear him shouting from his room. I walked down the corridor and went in. His mood was foul, and the staff was the target of his invective. I told him to behave and that I'd get him home.

I called the limo service and arranged a pickup at 5:30 P.M. I called Anita, awakened her, and picked her up at the lodge. The "luxury limo" was a van—granted, it was a large one—waiting at the clinic's back door.

I informed the folks in the white suits that all was ready and asked how they would get Hunter from the bed to the van. "Don't worry," they assured me. "We know how to do this and we really want him out of here." Five minutes later, four guys in full biohazard suits, including face shields, showed up with a gurney. Enduring curses and threats from Hunter, they lifted him from the bed to the gurney and wheeled him to the exit. Lifting his butt and broken leg, they placed him in the van. Anita boarded, and I got in my car and followed the van to I-70. We were on our way to Woody Creek.

We'd traveled one mile west when the van signaled to exit. More trouble? I followed it to the parking lot at McDonald's. I approached, and Hunter said that he wanted grilled cheese sandwiches. This item isn't on the McDonald's menu, so Anita taught the Bulgarian manager and Mexican cooks how to make them.

With a new cast, a bag of comfort food, and Owl Farm on the horizon, Hunter was once again in control of his environment, a basic requirement for Doc. My only problem, and Hunter's, was how we were going to get him and his cast from the van into the house. I called Deputy Joe DiSalvo and he agreed to borrow a wheelchair from the hospital and meet us at the farm. I called Cleverly. With grunting and screaming, we got Hunter into the chair, up the stairs, and into the kitchen, where he saw his four-foot-high stool on wheels. "Get me into the stool," he commanded. None of us thought the stool or Hunter was stable enough, but he demanded, and we complied. Once in place and safely home, he looked at his TV, which had been on for ten years, and said, "Hot damn! The Broncos are on *Sunday Night Football*. I'll take them and give three." Joey, Mike, and I took the bet, won, and never got paid.

The broken leg in Honolulu was a milestone in the downward spiral of Hunter's health. Hunter had become more and more sedentary over the years, but because he was gifted with the physique of a natural athlete, the accompanying atrophy had been gradual and subtle. The break was a large and immediate change in his life. Hunter had always been perfectly happy to be waited on; he was great at being lazy. For many years that seemed okay, because not getting off his ass was his choice; now he had no choice. He loved riding motorcycles. He loved shotgun golf, jumping into the Shark and flying down to the Tavern. He loved chasing women, literally chasing them, with the women running, and Hunter running. Now he was stuck in a chair and, worse, there was the regimen of physical therapy. To say Hunter wasn't one for regimens of any kind would be a massive understatement, and the therapy was painful hard work as well.

The situation Hunter found himself in would have depressed the most stoic of individuals, and I don't think Hunter was ever described as stoic.

Wednesday, February 16, 2005

It was a February Wednesday. Aspen was at 90 percent occu-
pancy, good for the mercantile interests, waitresses and waiters,
ski instructors, and everyone in the trickle-down cascade of resort economies.

"Marky Mark" and "Big Wave Dave," two surfers from Santa
Barbara, were in Aspen for a few days of skiing. They were staying at the St. Regis, one of Aspen's premier hotels, located at the
base of the mountain. Mark, with a day job in commercial real
estate, had helped DeDe, my sweetheart, to invest in a former
aircraft assembly plant out on the coast. DeDe was happy when
she flipped the property at a large profit. Their friendship had
endured. He invited us for dinner at a hip new bistro in an old

building on Hopkins Street. The food was good, and every seat was filled. Midway through our main course, "Big Wave" said that he and Mark had read everything that Hunter Thompson had written, admired him greatly, and asked if it might be possible to meet him during their short stay. I said that I'd call him after dinner.

Over the years I had fielded hundreds of requests to introduce people to Hunter. The Doc's phone numbers were not published, but mine were. It was common knowledge that Hunter and I were friends, and pilgrims from all over the world thirsted for a one-on-one audience with him. Some fans had even called me at 911. I vetted most of these requests by getting some details and a callback number, but I rarely bothered Hunter with this litany of suitors. I even treated friends' requests to hang out with Hunter as a general annoyance and imposition on him and rarely showed up with company. If I asked him if it was okay to bring somebody he would rarely decline, and I avoided abusing his hospitality.

Still, I liked my new friends and told them that if Hunter was up and about, not jamming on a deadline, a postprandial drive to Woody Creek might be in the cards. Just before dessert was delivered, my cell phone lit up. "Hi, it's Bob," I answered. "Bob, Hunter. What are you doing?" "Well, Hunter, I'm in town at dinner with DeDe and two dudes from California who are huge fans of yours." "Well, think they would like to come over?" "Yeah, I do. See you in half an hour."

We left the bistro. Mark and Big Wave picked up a bottle of ancient single malt that I would have had to take out a loan to pay for, and we headed to Woody Creek by the back road. I told our friends that I could not predict what kind of experience we were in for. DeDe knew why I was delivering this disclaimer.

Hunter could be warm and affable, rattlesnake mean, or unconscious. Buy the ticket . . .

We filed into the kitchen. Hunter was perched and fully dressed—a good sign. Introductions were made. Hunter hugged me and then hugged DeDe, while grabbing her ass. Normal welcome.

The next three hours were animated and fun to watch. Dave and Mark were extroverts. They submitted to Hunter's journalist interrogation and proved their knowledge of politics and sports. They felt comfortable in the strange world of Owl Farm. Hunter asked them if they would read from his works. On the kitchen counter were five or six of his books, each earmarked with sticky notes, and Hunter picked one up, opened it to a certain passage, and handed it to Dave. Dave began reading.

Hunter loved to hear his writings read aloud. During these readings he would look into the void, as if he were at a symphony or a jazz concert, and he would rock to the cadence of his words. He had hand signals that told the reader to slow down, read louder, read faster, or whatever Hunter thought would benefit his words. He was a conductor. If a reader mispronounced a word or left out a word—a word perhaps written twenty-five or thirty years earlier—Hunter would look up and ask, "Are you sure that's what I wrote?" Hunter knew. Like a mathematician with his unique formulae, Hunter *was* his writing. I had ceased being amazed years before, but Mark and Dave were impressed.

In the ensuing hours, Hunter was on his game. We were all laughing, and the room was saturated with mutual respect and an apparent joy for life. I had been aware of stress in Hunter's life. His business and his relationship and his health were all bothering him. Over the previous weeks, I'd answered his summonses many times. We had discussed possible solutions to various problems as he identified them. During these days we were always alone and often sat in the living room by the fire. One-on-one dialogues with Hunter were rare, precious, and revealing. With me, Hunter shed most of his paranoia and privacy. I would digest what he said and offer my thoughts and experiences without reservation. These exchanges were intimate, adult, and emotional. Over the years, we had shared such moments, and they had drawn us closer. I felt that I was able to assess Hunter's moods. On this Wednesday night, I thought Hunter's mood seemed perfect.

At about one in the morning, I said that I had to go to work early on Thursday. Dave and Mark wanted to ski but would probably have spent all night reading and talking. We said good night and got in my car. On the way into town we all felt that we had experienced a night of vintage Hunter. It was a small group with good chemistry, and now each of us is forever bound to the others by the fact that it was the last time any of us saw HST alive. On Sunday, Hunter took his life. Mark and Dave have a story to tell. Hunter loved stories. Long after that final, fatal Sunday, I still reflect on that Wednesday evening and wonder if it was a gift from Hunter, or a last gift from Hunter.

Cleverly

The week before Hunter died, our old friend Loren Jenkins was in town. That Wednesday, Loren and I met with Hunter at Owl Farm. We had a terrific afternoon; we solved many of the problems of the world and conspired to create new ones. When Loren and I hooked up the next day we agreed that it had been a fine time. Hunter at his best. I would have remembered that afternoon fondly, no matter how much longer Hunter had lived.

I was over at Hunter's again two days later. He was in excellent spirits. It was just the two of us. Anita had gone to the movies with her friend Sue. We talked about John Belushi. I had brought him up for some reason. His brother-in-law, Rob Jacklen, had lived in Aspen in the wild old days and we had both known him.

Hunter, of course, was close to John. We watched a basketball game. It was a rerun, but I didn't know that. Hunter had watched it a couple of evenings before. He made me gamble—game bet, proposition bets, the works. I wasn't doing very well. I wasn't suspicious; he'd usually win even when he wasn't bothering to flimflam me. Basketball is not my game.

Hunter had a lot of irons in the fire. The high-end art publisher Taschen was releasing a new edition of *The Curse of Lono*, first published in 1983. Ralph Steadman had done spectacular color illustrations for it, but the original edition hadn't come close to doing them justice. Hunter and Ralph had always felt slightly betrayed by this, so the new edition was a big deal. Hunter himself was working on an article for *Playboy* on Sean Penn's remake of the film *All the King's Men*. Penn and Hunter were good friends, and Doc had recently returned from New Orleans where the film was shooting. Hunter and I were schem-

Courtesy of Deborah Fuller

The great Ralph Steadman and Cleverly; a classic kitchen evening.

ing up a sequel to my 2002 *Sex and Death* calendar. Hunter was sure that Taschen would want to be involved in a project of such profound artistic merit. We were obliged to study dirty pictures as research. Hunter had other stuff in the works, too.

Physically, Hunter felt pretty crappy. He was coming back from a series of medical problems, and it was a very slow, painful process. I honestly thought that he was improving. You could tell by the griping that he was making an effort. Physical therapists were coming and going from Owl Farm regularly; sometimes debauchery and sin had to be put off. That evening Doc really seemed to feel okay.

So that last night was business as usual to me. We drank a bit, did a little of this, a little of that. At the end of the game, Hunter came clean about it being a rerun. He pointed at the screen. "See that tiny logo up in the corner?" I made my way over to the TV and put my nose up to the screen. It read, "Instant Classics." "What does it mean?" I asked. "It means I watched this game two nights ago." He forgave my debts and my stupidity. Who knows if he'd conned me before and not 'fessed up? If he had, his admission that night might have been telling. We'll never know.

Anita and Sue got home some time after eleven. They were bubbly and chatty; it had been a good movie. Eleven can be getting late for me, but it was always considered early at Owl Farm. I would leave soon.

A couple of days after Hunter's death I was quoted in a news story as saying that I would have been less surprised if he'd shot me. That was true. I had no idea. Woody Creek has never been considered an epicenter of mental health. It took a personality as large as Hunter's to actually stand out. There were always plenty of nutcases running around the neighborhood, but Hunter was never one of them. If I had been told that someone was going to do himself in, I could have made a list, but Hunter would have been at the bottom.

Not every evening at Owl Farm was a party. In recent years the kind of behavior that Hunter's young fans found so appealing was less and less frequent. An average night would more likely have been Hunter and a close friend or two discussing politics or some other current event. Serious and sober middle-aged guys doing what middle-aged guys do. This would on occasion be a disappointment to some fan who had gained admission, expecting to see a Bill Murray or Johnny Depp version.

Hunter worked. He had been producing a weekly column for ESPN for some time. He always had a book deal going, usually involving more than one expected volume. Then there were magazine pieces. It's pretty hard to keep a lot of balls in the air if your hands are full of something else.

People are still reading Hunter, as they have been for decades. I don't know if his books have ever gone out of print. One reason people read him is because he was very funny. He was very funny because he was very smart and because he was very honest. Hunter was a sixty-eight-year-old man who spoke to young people. He was a boozer and druggie who spoke to people who never embraced booze or drugs themselves. And he was a liberal who spoke to people whose political leanings were far away from his own. We all recognized that there was something in Hunter that we could only hope to see in ourselves: an utter lack of hypocrisy. When Hunter was being brutally honest with those around him it could sometimes be unpleasant, but he was just as honest about himself. He didn't sugarcoat it. In that sense he didn't play favorites.

I announced that I was leaving. "What do you mean you're leaving?" "It's late, Doc. I've had enough; the girls are back.

They can minister." He wasn't happy. The idea of being outnumbered by two effervescent females clearly didn't appeal. Anita and Sue came back into the kitchen, we made some small talk, and they wandered into the living room. "Okay, Doc. I'm outta here." I hollered goodnight to the gals. Hunter, giving me the stink-eye. "Fuckyoufuckyoufuckyoufuckyou." I walked through the Red Room smiling and waving goodnight. "Fuckyoufuckyoufuckyou . . ."

The next day I saw Sue. "How much longer did you stay?" I asked. "Only about ten minutes. We read for a bit then he called me a fucking bitch and told me to get the hell out." We laughed. No offense meant, no offense taken. The perfect end to a delightful night at Owl Farm.

By the following evening our friend was gone.

A February Sunday evening. Me, the cats, and the woodstove, not much happening, perfect. There's a knock on the door. My friend and neighbor Joe Fredricks is standing there, and I let him in.

Joe plows my driveway. I give him a piece of art, and he plows all winter. He'd gladly do it for nothing, but I'm flattered that he likes my stuff, so I don't mind coughing up. He plows Hunter's, too, and in the summer takes care of any heavy equipment at Owl Farm. Joe is also a Hunter buddy and attends all the major events.

This Sunday night drop-in is unusual. Joe is a volunteer fireman and has a scanner in his truck. A gunshot has been reported at an address on Woody Creek Road. We don't recognize the street number and try to figure out whose place it might be. That a gunshot in this neighborhood should be reported at all is a bit strange; it's Woody Creek, after all. We figure out nothing, and Joe decides to cruise down toward Hunter's and report back. I wait with limited interest.

Minutes later the phone rings. It's the sheriff. He's at Owl Farm. He gives me the news. Joe returns, and I tell him that I've heard. We have a couple of shots of tequila. The dispatcher on the scanner had the address wrong.

I didn't go out for the next few days. I didn't want to be underfoot at Owl Farm. But when I finally left the house, that's where I went. Hunter's family and his closest friends did the same, hunkered down. There were people less close to Hunter who hung at the Tavern holding court and giving interviews.

Some of us gave phone interviews—the press was going to talk to someone; better, we thought, people who really cared for Hunter than some rummy at the bar. All the time between Hunter's death and when I finally went over to Owl Farm I very much wanted to be there, to see Anita, Juan, and Jennifer. As soon as I got there, all I wanted to do was leave. I'm not exactly sure why; maybe because being in the house made it official. I'd never be in the kitchen with Hunter and our friends again.

So my visit that evening was brief. The next day I finally had to go out for provisions. The *Aspen Daily News* was sitting on the counter at the liquor store with a full-page picture of Doc. Seeing it did something to my chest I'd never felt before. When I got home there were sixty new messages on my machine.

During the next few days, patterns began to emerge. I'd stop by Hunter's intermittently; friends would drop off food there, the frenzy at the Tavern settled down, and the phone stuff tapered off. There was security all over Owl Farm. Guys taking themselves really seriously, which was their job, I guess. I wondered what Hunter would have thought.

From the evening of his death, those closest to Hunter wanted to get together for something small and informal. My favorite idea was to gather at Bob Rafelson's house and order a bunch of pizza. That had legs for a couple of days, but as time passed things inevitably got bigger, until at one point there was the thought of having a "come one, come all" at an Aspen nightclub. Bob Braudis felt that was a spectacularly bad idea and a recipe for chaos on a biblical scale. Bob Rafelson's voice got low and serious. "I've seen these things," he said. "There'll be helicopters; there'll be no way to control it." The man charged with public safety emerged. Sheriff Braudis suggested that people clear their heads and try again.

A couple of days later I was alone in the kitchen with Juan and he gave me a handwritten list. He said there was going to be a very private memorial at the Hotel Jerome a couple of weeks hence. He explained that the guest list didn't include everyone Hunter had ever known or worked with, just the friends he saw and called regularly, and with that in mind, he wanted my opinion. The list was several pages long. Hunter liked to call a lot of people. I added a few names, people I knew had either canceled trips or were flying in, to be here for whatever sort of memorial did happen. I also mentioned that I thought I owed it to Hunter to personally bring as many beautiful women as I could round up. Juan concurred.

The gals I usually hang out with were all on Juan's list anyway, so I was free to bring any date(s) I wanted. Despite my glib comment to Juan about herds of beautiful women, I really wasn't in the mood for that kind of hunt. I ended up taking Kallen, one of the great beauties from the golden age of the Jerome, an old friend whom I now saw rarely, a good example of the people who had been close to Hunter in the seventies and eighties but who had fallen away in recent years. She wasn't on the list. Anita had never met Kallen but knew of her from a famous photograph of Hunter, Kallen, and other luminaries taken at Doc's end of the bar at the Jerome back when that was the place to be. Anita was glad that she was going to get to meet Kallen at last.

I stopped by Kallen's place of work to discuss some details. We figured stuff out, and then she went on to tell me that she had channeled Hunter the evening before. "I beg your pardon? Channeled?" She told me how she and a friend had hooked up with Doc in the hereafter and proceeded to relate the conversation and revealed new and interesting facts. Naturally, I was pretty excited that my date had spoken to my dead friend. This was an unforeseen development. I gave Kallen a peck goodbye, and for the next few days imagined a number of scenarios in which Kallen broke the "channeling" news to Anita during the memorial, with tears, anguish, and general hysteria ensuing. I was not looking forward to witnessing any of those scenes being played out.

The event was nearing, and I was sitting with Anita trying to figure out how to tell her about this "chatting with the deceased" situation. I wasn't having much luck. Finally I just started in. "Listen Anita, I have to tell you something." I proceeded, with much trepidation, to lay out the channeling thing as I understood it. When I finished, I looked at Anita and this huge smile was spread across her face; she was beaming. "Me, too. I channeled Hunter just last night!" she gushed. I realized I had nothing to worry about. Clearly she and Kallen would get along just fine.

The memorial at the Jerome looked as much like a Hollywood red carpet event as a gathering for a man of letters; the celebrity count was over the top. In addition there was plenty of local security plus Secret Service guys with wires in their ears, all there to prevent anything unpleasant from happening to the big-name politicians. It was a mixed crowd.

There was an open bar, of course, and a beautiful buffet in the middle of the ballroom. I'd never seen so many intelligent, successful, talented people so wasted. These truly were Hunter's friends. As an Oscar-winning actor was passing through the buffet, he noticed a pair of feet sticking out from under the tablecloth. He grabbed the ankles and dragged out a local reporter, obviously a Thompson buddy. The reporter didn't come to until the next morning. He was disconsolate for days at having missed so much of an excellent party. Laila Nabulsi, a Hollywood power player, producer of *Fear and Loathing in Las Vegas,* and one of the best women in the world, introduced me to a handsome actor. We found some chairs and sat down and talked and drank. Purely by coincidence, every woman in the building who had previously met me for at least five seconds came over to say hello and see how I was doing. It was lucky timing; they also got to meet the actor. Yeah, he had an Oscar, too.

There were speeches, lots of speeches. Historian and author Doug Brinkley was the de facto MC and kept things moving along. There'd be a break after every two or three speeches so people could hit the buffet, bar, head, whatever. There were touching speeches; there were funny speeches; and that evening, some of the most articulate people I knew were so fucked up they could barely work their lips. The speeches were a mixed bag.

The event was scheduled to end at ten or eleven, and there were two or three after parties scheduled. One person had rented out an entire restaurant, one of the "inner circle" was having people down to his house, and there was something else at a local night spot. Two of them never happened. The Jerome was so good no one left. It was still going when I lurched off at 2:00 A.M. People did eventually head down to the friend's house and party till dawn, but without me. I dropped Kallen off and considered myself extremely lucky to make it home. I was almost in the sack when the phone rang. It was a beautiful woman I had met during the course of the evening, asking me where the party was. Every man on planet Earth knows there's only one answer to that question. But Genius gave her directions to the party.

When Johnny Depp arrived in Aspen for the Jerome memorial he was carrying something large. When Sheriff Braudis saw it he commented, "That must be interesting to travel with." Depp replied, "Hunter was interesting to travel with."

Almost from the beginning there had been scuttlebutt about a blastoff. There was talk of using one of the cannons from the ship in *Pirates of the Caribbean,* and the *Aspen Daily News* actually sponsored a contest for people who owned cannons. They were to send in a videotape of their cannon and explain why theirs should be the one to send Hunter off. There was also a rumor that something was already being fabricated in L.A. All this was engendered by a scene in a BBC documentary in which Hunter talked about, and even described, a cannon that would shoot his ashes into space. The scene was included in the boxed set of *Fear and Loathing in Las Vegas* and was also in Wayne Ewing's documentary *When I Die.* In the end, there was no need for the contest. Depp had been carrying an architectural model; behind it was a curved diorama almost four feet high and about as wide. The model was of a tall stainless-steel column, the top of which turned into a dagger and a giant gonzo fist. It sat on a contoured topography of rolling fields with little scale-model people; in the background on the diorama were mountains and sky. The people were tiny, to scale; the actual thing would have been enormous. The scale-model people were gazing up in awe at the fist, and some were taking pictures. There was an actual presentation that went along with the model. It plugged in and you turned it on. There was a large piece of silk that shrouded the entire column. The music started and as someone slowly pulled the silk off the fist, the music changed and suddenly the peyote button lit up and began to change colors. The music changed, the colors changed and whirled; it was all very theatrical, very impressive. Word on the street, Woody Creek Road, was that Johnny Depp had pledged four million dollars to the project. None of us had ever been to a four-million-dollar party.

In fact, the monument was to be 153 feet high, a little taller than the Statue of Liberty. One person noted that there probably weren't any buildings that tall between Denver and Salt Lake City. When the "fist" went from rumor to reality, there were lots of questions. Was this thing to be permanent? If so, did rural Woody Creek want to live with such a thing? If so, how did Pitkin County, the most regulated county on the planet, feel about it? Was it so tall as to pose a danger to aircraft? There were meetings, lots of meetings. What about the blastoff itself? One of the most prestigious fireworks companies in the country was contracted, people who do things at the Washington Monument. Colorado had been in a drought for years. Wildfires were springing up all over the Southwest every summer, and every summer it was touch and go whether the sheriff could allow the Fourth of July fireworks display on Aspen Mountain. What about burning down Woody Creek?

It was spring when these questions arose and Johnny Depp's front man arrived in town. The event planner, a relentlessly officious twit, showed up at his first meeting with county officials wearing an Armani suit. This didn't impress the guys in jeans and cowboy boots. You don't get to be an upper-level Hollywood suck-up by being totally unconscious, so he got with the dress code pretty quick. His Armani attitude remained, though. News of the blastoff spread and was picked up by the media. To say that the guest list was exclusive, a hard ticket, was something of an understatement. What of Hunter's legions of fans? The more ardent of them had had no respect for Hunter's privacy when he was alive and dangerous; there was no reason to expect any from them now. Anxiety was abroad in the land.

The event planner thought a Jumbotron, the kind of huge screen you see in football stadiums, could be set on the mesa across Woody Creek from Owl Farm. They'd just build a road where there had been none, erect a huge screen, truck in lots of porta-potties . . . you get the idea. Important people on one side of Woody Creek at the event, the unwashed masses on the other side. He approached a member of the Craig family, who owned that property. His pitch was pretty poor. He tried to wow them with dollar signs and celebrity name-dropping. Gee! They'd even get a whole free road out of it. The Craigs had a good deal of affection for Hunter, and probably would done what they could purely out of that affection, but they couldn't have cared less about Hollywood celebrities and Hollywood money. They had no need for a free road to nowhere.

The Jumbotron idea then migrated to Buttermilk Mountain. This was a little more realistic. The base of Buttermilk had been used for Jazz Aspen concerts and had seen tents, screens, and porta-potties before; there was precedent. Unfortunately, once you start talking about something like that, the bureaucrats really get into things with both feet. It takes about a year of bureaucratic wrangling to erect a birdhouse in Pitkin County. The hope that something of this nature could be pulled together in time was basically pie-in-the-sky. The Jumbotron idea was scrapped, and there was also no live feed to a local nightclub, as had been proposed toward the end of things. Ultimately, all that was done for any Hunter hunters who might have made the pilgrimage was a few porta-potties across from the Tavern. The Sheriff's Department, city and county officials, and the local papers took every opportunity to broadcast the fact that it was a private event and that no one was welcome.

The other issues remained. It became clear that all but Hunter's most loving neighbors might have a problem with a permanent tourist attraction. Especially considering the type of tourists it was likely to draw. It seemed that permanence wasn't feasible. As soon as the monument became a temporary structure, a lot of things got easier. Zoning and building permits were no longer a big issue. If aircraft couldn't avoid the thing for a bleeping week, screw them. As far as a special event permit went, people in Aspen had parties with hundreds of guests all the time. The fireworks and possible torching of Woody Creek were still on people's minds. The fireworks company sent a representative to hunker down with the Aspen Fire Department. Together they came up with a plan that was pretty much workable even if it never rained again. The plan involved mowing the meadow around the monument, soaking it, tankers full of water on hand, pyrotechnics that would be extinguished long before they came close to the ground, and more. Fortunately, there was rain the week before the event, and any lingering concerns there might have been about conflagration were laid to rest.

There were signs of life in the field behind Owl Farm toward the end of July. First, just a stake with an orange ribbon tied around it. Then workers began to repair the old rail fence and installed a steel ranch gate. Gravel was trucked in, and a road was built back up into the field. A large area was leveled off and covered with more gravel. Minor repairs were made to the entrance of Owl Farm, and security stations were created at that entrance and the entrance to the field. A new group of L.A. guys showed up. These were the people who were responsible for seeing that the thing got built. They were the polar opposite of the event planner and his crew of self-important weenies. Regular guys, they would work out in the "field of gonzo" all day and then head into Aspen at night to show folks how they partied in L.A. I have no idea how they made it through the summer.

A gigantic crane arrived, then generators and other heavy equipment. I encountered the first truck when I was coming out of the Woody Creek post office. A flat-bed semi, the biggest I'd ever seen, was stopped in front, the driver scratching his head, lost. With several huge cylinders as a load, it could only be one thing. You could see where the wrapping had pulled away from one of them that they were stainless steel. Another neighbor of Hunter's offered to lead the driver to the site.

With the arrival of the crane and tower components came the serious security. Dressed in black T-shirts with badges silk-screened on them and black jeans, they were stationed at the Owl Farm driveway and the new gate at the entrance to the field. They were mostly good-natured local guys who stayed cheerful despite the boredom and, I suspect, minimal compensation. The rare gawker seemed to annoy them a lot less than the supercilious event planner, who would go flying through the security checkpoint kicking up clouds of dust, without a glance of recognition for them.

The tower itself was wrapped around the vertical structure of a large stationary crane, the kind you see in the construction of skyscrapers. The cylinders were open in the back so they could slide around it; there were lots of them, many semi loads; each section weighed a couple of tons. Another crane on tracks stacked them, and then they were bolted in place. That crane was contracted out of Glenwood Springs. With the Glenwood guys and the L.A. guys, there were usually thirty or so people in the field. People wore GONZO MONUMENT TEAM T-shirts, très chic, and a very hot item to possess. The whole thing was cloaked in as much secrecy as possible, considering it was taking place in an empty field next to the road. At the end of the day, everything was draped with a huge blue tarp. When the last section, the fist itself, arrived, a special tent was erected just to conceal it while various technicians prepared it for installation.

The fist was finally set in place, and the tarps were replaced with one large piece of parachute fabric. Someone suggested that it resembled a giant penis wearing an ill-fitting condom. A lot of us were a little uncomfortable with the notion that there was a 150-foot-high penis in the neighborhood and tried to ignore it.

It seems that the actual unveiling was a complicated technical problem. In the model presentation, someone's hand would represent a helicopter and, while making helicopter sounds, would simply slip the drapery up and off the little monument. Considering the elegance of the model itself, this was clearly the lowest-tech aspect of that presentation. For some reason the chopper idea was scrapped. I don't know if the reason for this was aesthetics or safety, or logistics. The alternate solution was a deep secret, and it seemed to me to cause of a fair amount of anxiety in the people who were responsible for making sure it worked. A dress rehearsal was out of the question, as it would expose the monument and because the fabric was so light that there probably wasn't going to be much of it left intact afterward.

During the last week of monument assembly, another crew showed up. This group was constructing the platform upon which the party tent was going to sit. It was a big platform, a big tent. There were about four hundred guests, and it could probably have accommodated twice that number. A circular driveway was built up to the tent, and a beautiful path was created from the front of the tent up to the monument.

As the date of the event grew closer, the begging and wheedling for invitations grew more and more frenzied. The ice guy offered to provide free ice. Electricians and carpenters offered their services. Women offered. . . . But either you were on the list or you weren't; spouses and significant others of the invited couldn't get in if they themselves weren't on the list. All this resulted in my swearing to God never to attend another event that had lists and security. Somehow I don't think I'll have to worry about being tempted to break that oath.

The event was to take place on a Saturday, and people started to show up in town on the Monday before. Friends of Hunter's who had left the valley, celebrities based on the coast, media, and Hunter groupies. It was very much old-home week in Aspen. People who hadn't gotten together in years were hooking up, and since they were all Thompson cronies, they weren't meeting in church. The first unofficial event I attended was a cocktail party on Tuesday evening, after which I found myself wandering the streets of Aspen trying to find my car at two in the morning. From then on it was one thing after another: luncheons, cocktail parties, and dinner parties. By the time Saturday came around, a lot of folks were ready for rehab and not another party. But they were Hunter's people; they were warriors and knew how to rise to the occasion.

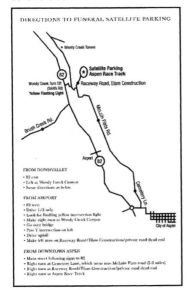

DIRECTIONS TO FUNERAL SATELLITE PARKING

Woody Creek Tavern

Satellite Parking
Aspen Race Track
Raceway Road, Elam Construction

Woody Creek Turn Off
(Smith Rd)
Yellow Flashing Light

Brush Creek Rd.

McLain Flats Rd

Airport

Cemetery Ln.

City of Aspen

FROM DOWNVALLEY
• 82 east
• Left at Woody Creek Canyon
• Same directions as below

FROM AIRPORT
• 82 west
• Drive 1/2 mile
• Look for flashing yellow intersection light
• Make right turn at Woody Creek Canyon
• Go over bridge
• Pass Y intersection on left
• Drive uphill
• Make left turn on Raceway Road/Elam Construction/private road dead end

FROM DOWNTOWN ASPEN
• Main street following signs to 82
• Right turn at Cemetery Lane, which turns into McLain Flats road (5.0 miles)
• Right turn at Raceway Road/Elam Construction/private road dead end
• Right turn at Aspen Race Track

It was a big deal even by Aspen standards. Parking on Woody Creek Road was absolutely forbidden by the county.

That week the media attention rivaled the frenzy of the days immediately following Hunter's death. As Saturday drew nearer, the attention became more intense. It ran the gamut from legitimate out-of-town reporters wanting appointments for interviews when they arrived in Aspen, to kids with video cameras claiming to be filmmakers working on documentaries. I felt kind of bad for the reporters. After all, Hunter was a journalist, and plenty of his journalist friends were going to be attending the event. The early plans included a "media pen" near the entrance to the field. I'd never heard of such a thing, and it sounded kind of demeaning to me, but I learned it was a common term and a common occurrence at fancy affairs. In any case, it would have been better than what actually did happen, which was nothing. The "media pen" idea was canned, and there was a total press blackout. Some of us gave interviews, hoping to compensate for the lack of access—kind of a booby prize. In the end you saw a lot of reporters interviewing each other at the Woody Creek Tavern on Saturday.

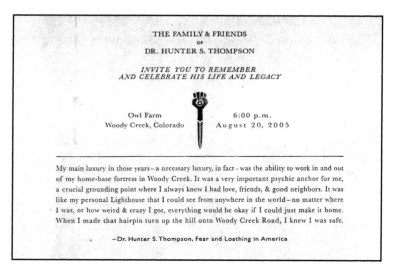

THE FAMILY & FRIENDS
OF
DR. HUNTER S. THOMPSON

*INVITE YOU TO REMEMBER
AND CELEBRATE HIS LIFE AND LEGACY*

Owl Farm   6:00 p.m.
Woody Creek, Colorado   August 20, 2005

My main luxury in those years – a necessary luxury, in fact – was the ability to work in and out of my home-base fortress in Woody Creek. It was a very important psychic anchor for me, a crucial grounding point where I always knew I had love, friends, & good neighbors. It was like my personal Lighthouse that I could see from anywhere in the world – no matter where I was, or how weird & crazy I got, everything would be okay if I could just make it home. When I made that hairpin turn up the hill onto Woody Creek Road, I knew I was safe.

– Dr. Hunter S. Thompson, Fear and Loathing in America

Many financial and carnal favors were offered for one of these.

The stepped-up security began on Friday night. County vehicles drove up and down, depositing orange cones and No Parking signs on both sides of Woody Creek Road. Leaflets were distributed to every house on the road, suggesting that people keep their dogs, cats, horses, cows, pigs, and Komodo dragons inside on Saturday night, as there were going to be bright lights and loud noises. The full security onslaught came first thing Saturday morning; it looked like the neighborhood was being overrun by the Viet Cong. Scores of part-time security people dressed in black from head to foot poured into Woody Creek. There were dozens at Owl Farm and dozens more at the entrance to the field; every house and driveway on the road had its own security person. For my security, I got a pretty, young, retired stripper named Sativa. I complained bitterly; I made her dinner. I told a number of friends that they could park in my driveway and walk to the tent. With Woody Creek in maximum-security lockdown mode, travel up and down our little country lane took on new dimensions. Was this what it was like trying to get from East to West Berlin? Parking in my driveway was a good option because the official parking was at the Woody Creek racetrack, four miles from Owl Farm, with limos constantly running back and forth. The folks at Flying Dog Ranch, Thompson friends and attendees of the event, also offered parking. A couple of miles up the road from my place, they hired a taxi to be on permanent duty shuttling guests to and from the party. As I said, it was an easy walk from my cabin to the party; making it back was a different matter entirely.

g r u p o a r i e s l. l. c

ATTENTION HOMEOWNERS

NOTICE OF UPCOMING SPECIAL EVENT IN YOUR AREA

Dear Neighbors,

On Saturday, August 20, 2005, the Thompson Family will be holding a special Hunter S Thompson Service that includes pyrotechnics at the Owl Farm in Woody Creek Valley.

Due to the nature of the pyrotechnics and the preservation of the animals in the area, we recommend that if you have animals to please make sure they are indoors after the hour of 5pm on Saturday, August 20th 2005. Horses especially should be placed in a secured indoor area by this time.

Please contact Vanessa Berlinsky, Event Coordinator at 818-439-4000 if you have any questions.

We appreciate your cooperation and patience with facilitating this event. Our apologies for the inconvenience.

grupo aries, l.l.c.

6220 hollymont dr. hollywood, 90068
917.375.8217

Johnny Depp's people did everything possible to be sensitive to Hunter's neighbors and the rural character of Woody Creek.

Several people took me up on my offer, among them my buddy Loren Jenkins and my date and her sister. My date was my date because she told me she was my date. A couple of weeks earlier she had come up to me and announced that she was going to be my date for the memorial. It was okay with me; she had her own invitation. When she mentioned that she was having a dress made in New York, was herself making up a batch of tincture of peyote and fresh coca leaves, and wasn't planning on wearing any underwear, the date idea really got some traction and I gave up any thought of arguing. I also figured I was pretty safe because her dad is one of my best friends.

Saturday evening came. There was a light rain. Loren, my first wife; Cass, our daughter; Eleanor; Eleanor's husband, Kuni; and a couple of others set out from my place. My "date" and her sister and dad were running late and would be along later. I told Sativa that anyone who tried to park in my driveway probably had my permission, and not to worry about it. We set her up out by the road with a lawn chair, cooler, and table.

The rain wasn't even substantial enough for us to put on the sweaters and jackets we'd brought against the cool Colorado evening to come. When we arrived at the entrance to the memorial site there were a couple dozen photographers set up across the street, most of them professionals with long lenses, some kids with little cameras. They obviously had to hike it from the Tavern, and I was glad to see that they weren't being hassled by the army of VC ninja security guys. The monument stood tall under the blue drapery. The road up to the tent passed in front of the entrance and circled back down. The walkway to the tent was festooned with banners with images of some of Hunter's favorite authors—Hemingway, Steinbeck—the whole thing had the trappings of a medieval joust.

It really was a big tent. There were an awful lot of people already there when we arrived, and it still seemed cavernous. Everything from the bar in the center to the furniture was draped in dark fabric: blues, purples, and black. Draped to the point that you couldn't really tell what was underneath. You couldn't tell that the bar was a bar or the couches and chairs were couches and chairs.

I was told that the guest list was the same as for the Jerome event, plus. The plus turned out to be mostly big-name Hollywood and Washington types who couldn't make that first service because of the short notice, and a few regular locals whose names had just slipped people's minds when the Jerome list was created. It was an impressive cast of characters. Since the bar was completely draped with mourning cloth, waiters and waitresses roamed around with mint juleps and bottled water. The drinks stopped being served when the speeches started. The oratory was a bit more lucid than at the Jerome affair. A lot of the same people spoke: family, Steadman, Doug Brinkley, and others, plus some really heavy-hitters like George McGovern. John Kerry was in attendance but didn't speak. The speechifying did go on, but it was impossible to get impatient when you considered the lineup.

As soon as the speeches were over people came out of nowhere and pulled off all the drapery to reveal what was essentially a huge set designed to look like Hunter's kitchen and living room. There were skulls, bats, stuffed animals, weapons, exact duplicates of the furniture and floor covering, even refrigerators like Hunter's, full of the beer and stuff Hunter's refrigerator was always full of. It was great. I heard it was the weasel event planner's idea, and I'll cheerfully give him credit if that's the case.

The entertainment was a mixed bag. A Japanese *taiko* drum band was playing from the time people started to arrive, and intermittently throughout the course of the evening. They had created a special piece in Hunter's honor. It was something, walking up the path to the tent with the exotic percussion echoing all around. I'd never heard anything like it before. Old Thompson friend jazz flutist David Aram played. Nitty Gritty Dirt Band alumnus and neighbor Jimmy Ibbotson played. Lyle Lovett got up on the stage with no introduction whatsoever and played a solo set. The stage for the music had its own tent just across from the front of the main tent.

The *taiko* band was the only music leading up to the blastoff. When the speeches ended and the drapery came off the furnishings, the bar opened and the drums started again. Waiters and waitresses came around with trays and made sure that everyone had a glass of champagne. It was clear that "it" was about to happen. The band stopped and "Spirit in the Sky" by Norman Greenbaum came on the loudspeakers. My friend George and I were sitting at a table toward the entrance side of the tent, the back of the tent as it faced the monument. Instead of shouldering our way through the crowd that was gathering toward the front, we went out the entrance and walked around. A couple of steps up and we were at the very front, standing next to Johnny Depp,

© Chloe Sells

Hunter becomes one with the zephyrs.

the best spot in the house. The music was loud and then louder. As it swelled, the drapery began to move and slowly rise up. It was actually being sucked down into a tube at the back of the fist. The whole scene was full Hollywood drama. Then the fist was completely revealed. Huge spotlights illuminated it, and the peyote button lit up, began to spin, and change colors. "Spirit in the Sky" boomed. This went on long enough for the entire effect to be absorbed.

And then the fireworks, which contained Hunter.

Apparently when one is cremated, the end product isn't that sandy stuff we see on TV. The result of real cremation is, for lack of a better term, a lot chunkier. For this reason, Hunter's remains had to be pulverized before they could be packed into the explosive canisters. This was done. Then a certain percentage of them was given to Juan and Jennifer, an equal amount to Anita, and the rest was shipped to the fireworks people in Florida. Doc was such a big guy that they had to use more charges than they had initially planned. The fireworks with Hunter imbedded in them traveled from Florida to Woody Creek in an armored car.

Johnny Depp's tribute to his friend.

So the peyote button spun and blinked and changed color, the music echoed across the valley, and what would have been Hunter's favorite part, the explosions, began. Shooting straight upward from the ground on both

© Chloe Sells

sides of the monument, and far higher, great colored streams of flame and light delivered what remained of Hunter S. Thompson into the ether above Woody Creek. I turned to George, "This is pretty swell, being here tonight, like this, but wouldn't we both trade it for one more night in the kitchen with Doc?" As George was agreeing, I felt a hand on my shoulder. It was one of the monument team guys. Standing directly behind us, he had tears rolling down his cheeks and he was nodding. All of those guys would have killed to have met Hunter just once.

The pyrotechnics ended and the party shifted into high gear, with the massive spotlights pointed at the monument creating three beautiful intersecting "gonzo fist" shadows on the low clouds that created a ceiling over Woody Creek. I thought of Hunter's last year, and his pain, and I thought that perhaps when we age and our senses become less acute, our vision and hearing dim, it's so that when we finally leave this world, we won't miss it so much.

—Michael Cleverly

Acknowledgments

In Hunter's books his acknowledgments came in the form of an Honor Roll, and to honor him we're going to continue that tradition. Hunter would never mention exactly what kind of contribution the honoree was being credited for; we expect that he did this to protect the guilty. Most of the people who have shared their memories and personal photographs with us are not included on the Honor Roll, as their contributions are enormous and obvious and can be seen throughout the text of the book, either as the subjects of their own chapters or with photograph credits. There are a few exceptions in which an individual's participation went beyond the sharing of stories and pictures.

HONOR ROLL

Andy Stone

Linda Lafferty

Randi Bolton

DeDe Brinkman

Deb Fuller

Heidi Mitchell

Stephanie Wells

Eleanor Takahashi

Kuni Takahashi

Oliver Takahashi

Cass Zajicek

John Zajicek

Hayden Cleverly

Tamara Tormohlen

Juan Thompson

Jennifer Thompson

William Thompson

Carol Craig

Simon Beriro

Tina Beriro

Jeff Hanna and the Nitty Gritty Dirt Band

Ed Hoban

Mary Harris

Shep Harris

Terry Helsing

Joe Fredricks

Paul Bresnick

Jeremy Cesarec

George Sells

Ziska Childs